IMPERIAL GERMANY

1871–1918

QUESTIONS AND ANALYSIS IN HISTORY

Edited by Stephen J. Lee and Sean Lang

Other titles in this series:

Hitler and Nazi Germany
Stephen J. Lee

The Weimar Republic
Stephen J. Lee

The French Revolution
Jocelyn Hunt

Parliamentary Reform 1785–1928
Sean Lang

The Spanish Civil War
Andrew Forrest

IMPERIAL GERMANY
1871–1918

STEPHEN J. LEE

ROUTLEDGE
London and New York

First published 1999
by Routledge
11 New Fetter Lane, London EC4P 4EE

Simultaneously published in the USA and Canada
by Routledge
29 West 35th Street, New York, NY 10001

Typeset in Grotesque and Perpetua by
Keystroke, Jacaranda Lodge, Wolverhampton
Printed and bound in Great Britain by
Clays Ltd, St Ives PLC

British Library Cataloguing in Publication Data
A catalogue record for this book is available from the British Library

Library of Congress Cataloging in Publication Data
Lee, Stephen J.
　　Imperial Germany 1871–1918 / Stephen J. Lee.
　　　　p.　cm. – (Questions and analysis in history)
　　Includes bibliographical references and index.
　　ISBN 0–415–18574–2
　　1. Germany–History–1871–1918. 2. Germany–History–1871–1918–
　　Study and teaching. I. Title. II. Series.
　　DD220.L.44　1998
　　943.08–dc21　　　　　　　　　　　　　　　　　　98–21784
　　　　　　　　　　　　　　　　　　　　　　　　　　　CIP

ISBN 0–415–18574–2

CONTENTS

Series preface   vii
Acknowledgements   viii

1   The formation and structure of the German Empire   1

2   Domestic policies, 1871–90   18

3   Foreign and colonial policies, 1871–90   37

4   Domestic policies, 1890–1914   54

5   Foreign and imperial policies, 1890–1914   71

6   Economy and society, 1871–1914   91

7   War and collapse, 1914–18   105

Notes   116
Bibliography   121
Index   124

SERIES PREFACE

Most history textbooks now aim to provide the student with interpretation, and many also cover the historiography of a topic. Some include a selection of sources.

So far, however, there has been no attempt to combine *all* the skills needed by the history student. Interpretation is usually found within an overall narrative framework and it is often difficult to separate the two for essay purposes. Where sources are included, there is rarely any guidance as to how to answer the questions on them.

The Questions and Analysis series is therefore based on the belief that another approach should be added to those which already exist. It has two main aims.

The first is to separate narrative from interpretation so that the latter is no longer diluted by the former. Each chapter starts with a background narrative section containing essential information. This material is then used in a section focusing on analysis through a specific question. The main purpose of this is to help to tighten up essay technique.

The second aim is to provide a comprehensive range of sources for each of the issues covered. The questions are of the type which appear on examination papers, and some have worked answers to demonstrate the techniques required.

The chapters may be approached in different ways. The background narratives can be read first to provide an overall perspective, followed by the analyses and then the sources. The alternative method is to work through all the components of each chapter before going on to the next.

ACKNOWLEDGEMENTS

Author and publisher are grateful to the following for permission to reproduce copyright material.

For written sources: G. Craig: *The Politics of the Prussian Army, 1640–1945* (Oxford 1955); W.N. Medlicott and D.K. Coveney (eds): *Bismarck and Europe* (London 1971); J.C.G. Röhl (ed.): *From Bismarck to Hitler. The Problem of Continuity in German History* (London 1970); *Memoirs and Letters of Sir Robert Morier* (London 1911); T.S. Hamerow (ed.): *Otto von Bismarck: A Historical Assessment* (Boston, Mass. 1966); P. Pulzer: *Germany 1870–1945* (Oxford 1997); W.M. Simon: *Germany in the Age of Bismarck* (London 1968); A.J.P. Taylor: *Bismarck: The Man and the Statesman* (London 1961); G.E. Buckle (ed.): *The Letters of Queen Victoria*, Vol. 3 (London 1930); M. Hurst (ed.): *Key Treaties for the Great Powers 1814–1914* (Newton Abbot 1972); T.S. Hamerow (ed.) *The Age of Bismarck. Documents and Interpretations* (London 1973); J.A. Nichols: *Germany after Bismarck. The Caprivi Era 1890–1894* (Cambridge, Mass. 1958); W. Carr: *A History of Germany 1815–1990* (London 1991); A. Fried and R. Sanders (eds): *Socialist Thought* (London 1964); T.A. Kohut: *Wilhelm II and the Germans: A Study in Leadership* (Oxford 1991); M. Balfour: *The Kaiser and his Times* (London 1964); G. Layton: *From Bismarck to Hitler: Germany 1890–1933* (London 1995); J.C.G. Röhl: *Germany without Bismarck* (London 1967); Sigmund Freud: *New Introductory Lectures on Psycho-analysis* (Harmondsworth 1979); J.C.G. Röhl: *The Kaiser and his Court* (Cambridge 1994); V.R. Berghahn and M. Kitchen (eds): *Germany in the Age of Total War* (London 1981); G. Martel: *The Origins of the First World War* (Harlow 1987); D.G. Williamson: *Bismarck and Germany 1862–1890* (Harlow 1986); V.R. Berghahn: *Modern Germany* (Cambridge 1982); S. Miller: *Mastering Modern*

European History (London 1997); L.L. Snyder: *The Weimar Republic* (Princeton, NJ 1966); A. Kaes, M. Jay and E. Dimendberg: *The Weimar Republic Sourcebook* (Berkeley 1994).

For illustrations used, acknowledgements are due to the following: Bildarchiv Preussischer Kulturbesitz, Berlin; AEG Firmenarchiv, Frankfurt; Der wahre Jakob.

1

THE FORMATION AND STRUCTURE OF THE GERMAN EMPIRE

BACKGROUND NARRATIVE

The German Empire (sometimes referred to as the Kaiserreich) was formally proclaimed in the Hall of Mirrors in the Palace of Versailles on 18 January 1871. This somewhat strange venue was a result of the way in which the new state was put together.

Before 1866 'Germany' had been a loose term. Its political form was the German Confederation, set up at the Congress in Vienna (1815) to replace the Holy Roman Empire – the so-called 'thousand-year Reich' which had been founded in the ninth century by Charlemagne and ended in 1806 by Napoleon. The German Confederation had comprised most of Prussia, the Austrian and Bohemian provinces of the Austrian Empire and thirty-nine smaller states which had their own rulers. The Confederation had a central Diet, or executive council, but no overall executive apart from the nominal presidency of Austria.

Before the late 1850s moves towards closer unity had been sporadic and unpredictable. One underlying impetus had been cultural, with the emphasis on a shared heritage and common linguistic identity greatly accentuated by the Romantic movement. Another trend had been an early alliance between liberalism and nationalism. In 1848 liberals allied to popular uprisings, overthrew the governments in Berlin, Munich and Vienna, and forced the election of the Frankfurt Assembly. This sought to establish a united Germany based on a progressive constitution, only to find the forces of counter-revolution, led by Austria, too strong: the scheme had therefore collapsed. A third force had been economic, with the growth of the Zollverein, or customs union, which had linked most of the smaller German states with Prussia but had excluded the whole of Austria.

There had, therefore, been long-term influences behind the emergence of a German state. But unification meant directing the cultural and economic flows into a more viable political channel. From the late 1850s the influence of Prussia increased. The impetus was accelerated rapidly by Wilhelm I of Prussia who began to think in terms of Prussian dominance over Germany in 1861. This involved doubling the Prussian army, and securing the approval of the Prussian Landtag (or parliament) for an increase of 400,000 men. The resulting constitutional conflict was won by Otto von Bismarck, appointed Minister President of Prussia in 1862. Over the next nine years Bismarck involved Prussia in three wars, during which the smaller German states were removed from the presidency of Austria, the German Confederation was dissolved and Prussia expanded to form a new and more fully integrated Germany. In retrospect the events from 1863 to 1871 seem to have led inexorably to German unity, although there has been some dispute among historians as to how much of this was intentional. This is examined in Analysis 1.

The outline chronology is as follows: the conflicts started in 1864 when Christian IX attempted to incorporate the neighbouring duchies of Schleswig and Holstein into his kingdom of Denmark. These had previously been under the rule of the Danish monarch but separate from the state of Denmark. Since Holstein was pre-dominantly German speaking, it received the support of a number of smaller German states. Prussia and Austria quickly entered the fray and sent troops to prevent the annexation. The outcome of a one-sided conflict was the Treaty of Vienna (1864), whereby the King of Denmark renounced all claim to the duchies. By the Convention of Gastein (1865) between Austria and Prussia, the former was to administer Holstein and the latter Schleswig.

This arrangement soon produced a conflict between Prussia and Austria. Prussian rule over Schleswig was far tighter than that of

Austria over Holstein; the result was an accusation that dissidents in Holstein were seeking to undermine Schleswig. In a dispute over the future of the two duchies, Prussia declared war on Austria in 1866, most of the smaller German states siding with the Austrians. Prussian armies quickly defeated Saxony, Hesse and Hanover, while the Austrians were defeated at Sadowa, or Königgratz, within six weeks. By the Treaty of Prague the German Confederation was dissolved and Austria gave up all claim to control within Germany. Prussia proceeded to annex both Schleswig and Holstein, as well as Hanover, and to convert the rest of the smaller states of north and central Germany into a new North German Confederation closely controlled by Prussia.

The three south German states of Bavaria, Baden and Württemberg were not included until 1871, when the North German Confederation was transformed into the German Empire. The catalyst for this was a third war, this time between Prussia – or the North German Confederation – and France. The traditional view is that Bismarck provoked the French Emperor, Napoleon III, into committing a series of diplomatic blunders, thereby alienating the south Germans who had initially looked to France for support against Prussia. In 1870 Bismarck rewrote and published a telegram sent to him by Wilhelm I of Prussia. In its edited version this gave the impression that Wilhelm had insulted the French government in his dealings with it about the possibility of the throne of Spain being occupied by a junior member of the house of Hohenzollern; this would have provided a link, however tenuous, with Prussia. Napoleon III, confident of victory, declared war on Prussia, only to see the French armies defeated at Metz and Sedan. He was forced to abdicate, and, by the Treaty of Frankfurt (1871), France surrendered Alsace and Lorraine to Germany.

The newly proclaimed German Empire was in theory a federation of autonomous, mostly monarchical states. In practice, it was dominated by Prussia, the king of which was also the Emperor, or Kaiser. The Minister President of Prussia was usually the Imperial Chancellor: until 1890 both positions were held by Bismarck. The extent of the liberal and authoritarian influence on the institutions of the Reich are examined in Analysis 2.

ANALYSIS (1): HOW WAS GERMANY UNITED?

The narrative answer to this question has already been provided. There are, however, two issues connected to these events which need to be analysed. First, was a united Germany actually planned by those who brought it about? And second, was Prussia necessarily the natural core for this unity?

There was for a long time a tendency to see the whole process of German unification as planned and systematic. Grant Robertson, for example, maintained that it was a 'marvellous march of events, in which each stage seems to slip into its pre-appointed place'. (1) The argument that unification was pre-planned may be summarised as follows: Bismarck helped precipitate the events which brought about unification. He involved Prussia in the war against Denmark. He insisted on the separate administration of Schleswig and Holstein which he later exploited to provoke a war with Austria in 1866. He then encouraged Napoleon III to make claims against the southern German states, Belgium and Luxembourg. At the same time, he developed a series of agreements to isolate Napoleon III, including a generous Treaty of Prague with Austria, a diplomatic accord with Russia over Polish refugees fleeing into Prussia, and an alliance with Italy (1866). He then manipulated the crisis over the Spanish candidature, knowing full well that his version of the Ems telegram would provoke Napoleon III into a declaration of war on Prussia. To an extent Bismarck himself started the myth. In 1862 he provided Disraeli with an outline of his intentions: 'When the army has been brought to such a state as to command respect, then I shall take the first opportunity to declare war with Austria, burst asunder the German Confederation, and give Germany a national union under the leadership of Prussia.' (2)

In the fullness of time this approach came to be strongly challenged as revisionist historians stressed that the whole process of unification was entirely fortuitous and not deliberately engineered by Bismarck. A.J.P. Taylor believed that German unity occurred *despite* Bismarck, who wanted no further war after that with Austria in 1866: 'In truth, the French blundered into a war which was not unwelcome to them: and Bismarck, though taken by surprise, turned their blunder to his advantage.' (3) Taylor denied that Bismarck had any blueprint or plan for German unity. It could certainly be argued that any of Bismarck's statements about his proposals for the future were sufficiently vague to lack the element of planning which a blueprint involves. That they were eventually fulfilled can therefore be seen as pure coincidence.

Additional evidence against the original 'intentionalist' argument comes from the diplomatic situation in Europe at the time. Unification was therefore due quite as much to the conjunction of uniquely favourable external factors as to the insight of Bismarck. What he did was to manipulate events as they occurred rather than shape them from the outset. The main external impediments to German unification had been the position of Austria and the attitudes of Russia and France. Austria had been severely weakened by the upheavals of the mid-nineteenth century. From 1815 her position in Germany and Italy had rested on close collaboration with Russia which, indeed, had helped put down the revolution of Hungary against Austria in 1848–49. But the Crimean War (1854–56) and consequent Russian defeat meant the withdrawal of Russia into a period of diplomatic isolation and the connection with Austria was cut. This coincided with an increase of Italian nationalism which resulted in a weakened Austria being driven from northern Italy by a combination of Piedmontese and French troops in 1860. Already undermined in Italy, Austria was not ideally placed to resist the march of Prussia in Germany. Meanwhile, France was being seen increasingly as the most likely aggressor in Europe. This was certainly the view of British statesmen like Palmerston, who were concerned at the prospect of French expansion at the expense of Belgium and Luxembourg, a scenario Palmerston had already helped to prevent while he had been Foreign Secretary during the 1830s. In the circumstances, therefore, Bismarck had to work no harder at discrediting and isolating France in Europe than he had over weakening the position of Austria in Germany. They were simply happening.

These represent the poles of interpretation. But there is a viable alternative. It is possible to combine the exigencies of the situation in Europe with the actions taken by Bismarck to develop a scenario in which unity was intended, but the measures taken were purely in response to the situations as they arose. The emphasis is therefore restored to Bismarck as interventionist – but primarily as a pragmatist and opportunist. Indeed, it seems that this is how he saw himself. He regarded events as part of an irresistible 'time stream of history'. He believed that 'One cannot make history.' It was, nevertheless, possible to be part of that time stream by understanding and manipulating events. 'Man cannot create the current of events. He can only float with it and steer.' (4) It was, however, essential to be able to pursue several strategies simultaneously. As one after the other was closed off by events the one that remained would appear to have been planned from the outset. Bismarck therefore tended to delay vital decisions until the situation was entirely clear – this enabled him to move history into one of the channels which had always existed as a possibility. This 'strategy of alternatives' is one way of understanding his dealings with Austria and France. In the case of Austria he followed several lines. He promoted an alliance in 1864; he followed this by the Convention of Gastein which, he hoped, would induce Austria to yield to Prussia the lion's share of control in northern Germany. If it did not, then the situation in Schleswig and Holstein could be used at some time in the future to precipitate a conflict between Austria and Prussia. Similarly, Bismarck followed several courses in his diplomacy with France. He kept Napoleon III friendly by vague hints of territorial gain in the area of the southern Rhineland. At the same time, he was in no hurry to complete unification with the south, hoping that this might be accomplished through peaceful means, possibly through the establishment of a common Federal Customs Council. Eventually, however, it became clear that Baden, Württemberg and Bavaria were too friendly with France for Bismarck's liking. He therefore used the diplomatic blunders of Napoleon III to drive a wedge between France and the south German states: he publicised Napoleon's demands for the Saarland and for Bavarian and Hessian territory in the Rhine area. He was not, however, convinced until 1870 that Prussia would benefit from war with France. The Hohenzollern candidature offered him the opportunity to bring to a head a crisis with France: one of the channels he had anticipated.

It is arguable, therefore, that German unification was intended but not planned. In which case was the Prussian base its most logical form?

In some ways it was not. Almost all the smaller German states supported Austria in the Confederation Diet over the constitutional crisis concerning Schleswig and Holstein in 1866. Many mobilised against Prussia and ended up united by conquest; some states, like Hanover, lost their separate identities altogether and ended up being absorbed into Prussia itself. In a sense, therefore, unification was imposed upon the smaller German states against their preference for a looser and more traditional association with both Prussia and Austria. The parliamentary approach to the problems of the 1860s favoured Austria. The military approach was Prussia's and the smaller states had to be brought into submission to Prussia, and Austria herself defeated.

Even then the process was incomplete and Bismarck faced the suspicion, even hostility, of the southern states; hence his delay in trying to incorporate them and the need to use Napoleon III's blunders.

It is sometimes argued that the southern states' continued preference for Austria was primarily for religious reasons. This may well have been the case with Bavaria, the population of which was predominantly Catholic. But Baden and Württemberg had strong Protestant traditions going back to the sixteenth-century Reformation. We should therefore be suspicious of this line of reasoning. It seems that it was a case of the south Germans being more wary of Prussia than feeling an attachment to Austria.

All this might appear to point to the Prussian initiative for unification being one which was entirely artificial and brutally imposed. In a sense this is what Bismarck said when he warned the Prussian Landtag in the Army Bill debate of 1862 that Prussian predominance in Germany must be based on military security. 'Germany looks not to Prussia's Liberalism but to her power . . . The questions of the day will not be decided by speeches and majority decisions . . . but by blood and iron.' (5) We could see this as a continuation of a traditional approach based on Prussian expansion within Germany rather than Prussian leadership over Germany. This had certainly been the aim of Frederick the Great (1740–86), who extended Prussia by absorbing Silesia and part of Saxony. Bismarck has often been seen as his natural successor; not being a 'German' nationalist, his premise was that 'Prussians we are and Prussians we shall remain.'

Yet it is possible to move so far in this direction that we can end up with the view that unification was entirely arbitrary, based simply on the whims of a Prussian expansionist. It makes more sense to see the connection between Germany and Prussia as being part of the broader flow of influences and events. Bismarck was certainly conscious of this link, although he felt that it had become unnecessarily complicated. Hence, in his own words: 'The Gordian Knot of German circumstances was not to be untied by the gentle methods of dual policy [but] could only be cut by the sword.' (6)

There is certainly plenty of evidence of long-term connections between Prussia and the idea of a more integrated Germany. It was to Prussia that the nationalists came increasingly to look, and in 1849 the Frankfurt Parliament decided to offer the crown of a united Germany to the King of Prussia. Nor did the collapse of the Frankfurt Parliament mean the end of this connection. Bismarck may have denied that Germany looked to Prussia for her liberalism, but German liberals continued to look to Prussia in the 1850s and 1860s as the more likely source of constitutional reform and genuine integration. As will be shown in Analysis 2, Prussia had a tradition of progressive change as well as one of military power.

Also of importance was the economic link between Prussia and Germany. Some have gone so far as to argue that unification was part of a long-term economic process. The first to stress the economic base for German unity was J.M. Keynes, who wrote in 1919, 'The German Empire was created more by coal and iron than by blood and iron.' (7) Recent historians like Böhme have adopted a similar argument, pointing to the inexorable influence of economic growth, dominated by Prussia. Two factors were particularly influential.

One was the gradual integration of the economies of the German states through the Zollverein. This united the various customs unions already in existence so that, by as early as 1834, the economies of the smaller German states had been linked with that of Prussia and severed from that of Austria. The other factor was the economic growth of Prussia, which had experienced the first industrial revolution in continental Europe. The opportunity was provided by the incorporation of the Rhineland and Westphalia into Prussia by the Treaty of Vienna in 1815: in these areas were some of the largest coal and iron-ore deposits in Europe. The Prussian government made the most of the new opportunities with the policies in the 1850s of such dynamic ministers as Manteuffel, von der Heydt and Delbrück. Coal and iron production more than doubled during this decade, while steel production rapidly expanded with the use of the newly developed Bessemer process. The Zollverein's exports increased from 357 million thaler in 1853 to 455 million by 1856. During the same three-year period Austria's fell from 184 million thaler to 150 million. Understandably, Austria wanted to replace the Zollverein by a broader Danubian customs union, but this was strongly resisted by Prussia. Indeed, Böhme sees in this the catalyst for the acceleration of the unification process: 'The quarrel over the Zollverein became of central importance for the development of the German question, and it can be asserted that the kleindeutsch national state arose chiefly from the Prussian defence against the economic order conceived by Austria for the great Central European region.' (8)

In overall conclusion two points need to be emphasised. First, a united Germany was not some aberration: it was intended, although it would be too much to claim that it was planned, step by step, by a supreme architect. Second, the links the German states had with Prussia contained forces which both repelled and attracted them. The final bond was created by force but this does not mean that it was an artificial one. The influence of Prussia had been both progressive and reactionary, a combination which was to persist throughout the history of the Reich.

Questions

1. Was the unification of Germany intended?
2. Was a united Germany simply an enlarged Prussia?

ANALYSIS (2): HOW AUTHORITARIAN WAS THE REICH?

The formation of the German Empire differed from the proposed unification by the Frankfurt Parliament in 1848–49 in that it was achieved from above, and by force, rather than from below, and by consent. Nevertheless, it did involve enthusiastic support from those who had once hoped for unification by parliamentary means. The new Reich therefore had both liberal and authoritarian principles. The key question concerns the balance in which these existed.

Liberal influences had been widespread throughout the German Confederation in the first half of the nineteenth century. Many of the smaller German states had taken the initiative in the 1848 revolutions by introducing progressive constitutions drafted by middle-class lawyers. Admittedly, Prussia had failed to take the lead expected of it by the Frankfurt Parliament. Nevertheless, the constitution which was introduced in Prussia in 1850 was one of the most progressive in Europe at the time and more than capable of being adapted to future liberal changes. Prussia had also seen a wave of reform in the late 1850s as Wilhelm, acting as regent for Friedrich Wilhelm IV, introduced a liberalising programme known as the 'New Era'. Prussia had therefore continued to appeal much more than Austria to German liberals. Indeed, many of Prussia's liberals had thrown in their lot with Bismarck after the failure of the earlier attempts at constitutional unity. They had achieved partial success in the constitution of the North German Confederation. This had provided a Reichstag, or central parliament, elected by male suffrage and therefore directly in line with the proposals made at Frankfurt in 1849.

The obverse side of German unity was a strong authoritarian tradition. This had always been apparent in the Prussian system of government and was something which Bismarck continued to regard as a virtue. His view was that political change must be kept under constraint. Hence, 'in order that German patriotism should be active and effective, it needs as a rule to hang on the peg of dependence upon a dynasty'. (9) He was also socially conservative and strongly opposed to any form of revolution. There has been a long continuity in the historiography of Bismarck here, especially among German scholars like Rothfels, Bussman, and Wehler. Wolfang J. Mommsen summarises the general aim of Bismarck as being to 'preserve the pre-eminence of the traditional elites despite the changes which were taking pace in German society. Bismarck's policies, in other words, were a defensive social strategy conducted on behalf of the ruling strata.' (10) It is hardly surprising that such influences were at their strongest in Prussia, just as it was Prussia which had so often taken the lead in introducing progressive reform.

The new Reich, therefore, had a split identity which mirrored that of Prussia. It comprised elements of liberalism and authoritarianism. How did these relate to each other in practice? Historians have differed over this. Some have argued that the constitution of the Empire was a proper consensus and that it therefore made a reality out of German unification. The alternative, suggested earlier in the twentieth century by Weber, was that the constitution was no more than a disguise for the predominance of a reactionary Prussia over the other German states. These two views provide the two ends of the spectrum. But between them come more subtle combinations of liberal and authoritarian influences.

The Second Reich was established as a federation. Each of its twenty-five states retained its own ruler and government, while being represented according to its size in the central Diet or Bundesrat. The smallest states had one seat each; Prussia, as the largest, had seventeen, which conferred the right of veto on any constitutional change proposed by the Bundesrat. On the positive side this went some way towards guaranteeing the autonomy which the smaller states felt they were losing to Prussia during the process of unification: this applied especially to the southern states of Baden, Bavaria and Württemberg. On the other hand, federalism was always a double-edged weapon. The elite within Prussia, especially the large landowners, or Junkers, actually preferred the federal system since it guaranteed the continued separate identity of Prussia, while the composition of the Bundesrat ensured Prussian control. Besides which, the members of the Bundesrat were appointed by the state rulers, not elected. In practice federalism meant that the Prussian government had indirect control over the other states without being diluted by them. For example, the King of Prussia was also the Kaiser, the Minister President of Prussia was usually also the Reich Chancellor, and the Prussian civil service set the pattern for the Reich – as opposed to individual state – administration.

The Reich executive comprised the individual state governments, the largest of which was Prussia. The Reich government was headed by the Kaiser who alone was responsible for the appointment and dismissal of the Chancellor. None of the Chancellor's cabinet was chosen from deputies serving in the Reichstag. This structure meant that some of the aims of the liberals in the 1860s were not met. There was no arrangement for the accountability of the Chancellor to the Reichstag – no equivalent therefore to the British Prime Minister's responsibility to Parliament. On this issue, the authoritarian approach based on maintenance of an unfettered executive triumphed. The executive was also firmly in control of foreign policy, the army and navy, the Kaiser acting as Commander-in-Chief. In this way the Kaiser's government had the ultimate sanction of the use of the army – a traditional authoritarian device which nullified the intentions of the liberals in the 1860s to demilitarise the political power structure of Germany.

A more promising appearance of progressive liberalism can be seen in the Reich's legislature. As in the period of the North German Confederation, the Reichstag was elected by universal male suffrage. Any legislation needed its assent, as did the military budget. The Reichstag was responsible for enacting a range of social and constitu- tional reforms, even during the administration of Bismarck, and was to prove capable of mounting some opposition to Bismarck and his successors on a number of occasions. On the other hand, the Reichstag had no formal influence over the composition of the executive and there was no tradition of party government in the Reich.

This was anomalous, since Germany had a wealth of political parties, formed from the late 1860s to the early 1870s. These ranged from the Conservatives, and their offshoots the Free Conservatives, through the two liberal parties – the National Liberals and the Progressives – and the predominantly Catholic Centre, to the Social Democrats on the left, who represented part of the newly enfranchised working class. Nowhere else in Europe was there such a complete representation of the interests of the different sections of the population. And yet these parties were to be continually frustrated in the relations with the executive, as Bismarck used and abused each one in turn. Deprived of any prospect of a share in government, each tended to pursue narrow aims based on the interests of its constituents which, in turn, made it less likely that any genuinely party-based government would evolve. Mommsen correctly describes the overall political system as 'a semi-constitutional system with supplementary party-political features'. (11)

The whole structure of the Reich came under a series of economic and social strains which in turn accentuated the conflict between liberal and authoritarian principles. Industrialisation created a wealthier middle class and an ever-expanding proletariat: both were out of sympathy with the traditional social elite, the Junker class, which was based on land ownership. There were also sectional differences based on religion or on ethnic minorities. The attempted resolution of the problems thrown up during the whole period of the Reich showed authoritarianism operating in a way which had to take account of liberal constraints. This happened in two stages. In the first Bismarck sought to maintain his authoritarian ascendancy by making various coalitions in the Reichstag in support of government policy. This is one of the themes of Chapter 2. After 1890 the regime of Wilhelm II sought to create mass support for the Reich through the pursuit of expansionist policies abroad. Both approaches – the manipulation of parties and the deliberate spread of nationalism to the lower classes – showed that while the governments of the Second Reich retained the initiative they were constrained in what they could do by pressures that they had to acknowledge and with which they had to deal.

The constrained authoritarianism which characterises the Reich was, according to Mommsen, the result of a series of 'skirted decisions'. Boldt, too, maintains that 'matters of sovereignty and government were deliberately left obscure'. (12) The underlying political culture was authoritarian but the existence of liberal influences meant that authoritarianism was never autocratic – either as in France under Bonapartism between 1852 and 1870 or as in Russia under the tsars up to 1917.

Questions

1. Did authoritarianism stifle liberal influences in the 1871 constitution?
2. 'A strong parliamentary system depends on effective political parties.' Did Germany have these?

SOURCES

1. PRUSSIA, AUSTRIA AND GERMANY

Source A: from a letter by Bismarck to Otto Manteuffel, April 1856.

Because of the policy of Vienna, Germany is clearly too small for us both; as long as an honourable arrangement concerning the influence of each cannot be concluded and carried out, we will both plough the same disputed acre, and Austria will remain the only state to whom we can permanently lose or from whom we can permanently gain. For a thousand years intermittently . . . the

German dualism has regularly adjusted the reciprocal relations of the powers by a thorough internal war; and in this century also no other means than this can set the clock of evolution at the right hour . . . In the not too distant future we shall have to fight for our existence against Austria and . . . it is not within our power to avoid that, since the course of events in Germany has no other solution.

Source B: from the speech by Bismarck to the Prussian Landtag, 29 September 1862.

Prussia's boundaries according to the Vienna treaties are not favourable to a healthy political life; not by means of speeches and majority verdicts will the great decisions of the time be made – that was the great mistake of 1848 and 1849 – but by iron and blood.

Source C: from Bismarck's *Memoirs*, published in the 1890s.

On 23 July [1866], under the presidency of the King, a council of war was held, in which the question to be decided was whether we should make peace under the conditions offered or continue the war . . . On this occasion . . . I declared it to be my conviction that peace must be concluded on the Austrian terms, but remained alone in my opinion; the King supported the military majority . . . I set out the following day to explain [that] we had to avoid wounding Austria too severely; we had to avoid leaving in her any unnecessary bitterness of feeling or desire for revenge; we ought rather to reserve the possibility of becoming friends again with our adversary of the moment, and in any case to regard the Austrian State as a piece on the European chessboard and the renewal of friendly relations with her as a move open to us. If Austria were severely injured, she would become the ally of France and of every opponent of ours; she would even sacrifice her anti-Russian interests for the sake of revenge on Prussia.

Source D: from a letter from Sir Robert Morier, a British diplomat in Vienna, to Lady Salisbury, 24 June 1866.

The one thing for which . . . above all other things, I conceive Bismarck ought to be execrated, is his having by the impress of his own detestable individuality on the political canvas now unrolling before Europe so utterly disfigured the true outlines of the picture, that not only public opinion, but the judgement of wise and thoughtful men is almost sure to go wrong . . . If Bismarck succeeds the world will clap its hands and say he was the only man who knew how to bring about what the world, which always worships success, will say was a consummation it always desired. Whereas that which will be really proved is that

Prussia was so strong and so really the heart and head and lungs of Germany, that she could, by her mere natural development WITH, instead of AGAINST, the liberal and national forces of Germany, have effected what required to be done by peaceful means and without bloodshed.

Source E: an assessment of Bismarck by the German historian Heinrich von Sybel in *The Founding of the German Empire*, published between 1890 and 1898.

He was not striving for world-dominion nor for boundless power, but for the means to secure and strengthen his Prussian Fatherland. So much acquisition of power and territory as was necessary for this he laid hold of with iron grasp – so much and no more. The intoxication of victory never disordered his judgement, nor got the mastery over his fixed principles of moderation.

Questions

*1.   (i)   What is meant by '. . . plough the same disputed acre . . .' (Source A)? (2 marks)

     (ii)   To which victory, over Austria in 1866, might Document E be referring? (1 mark)

    (iii)   By which treaty was the 1866 war between Prussia and Austria concluded? (1 mark)

2.   How effectively did Bismarck use language in Sources A and B to put across his ideas? (4 marks)

3.   In what ways did Bismarck's perception of Austria in Source C differ from that in Source A? (4 marks)

4.   How reliable would you consider Sources C and D as an assessment of Bismarck's aims and methods? (5 marks)

5.   How far do Sources A to D, and your own knowledge, lead you to agree with the opinions cited in Source E? (8 marks)

Worked answer

*1. *[Some questions on sources, usually the first, ask for an explanation of a specific reference. Where one mark is available, a word or phrase is expected; anything more than this would earn nothing extra. For two marks a slightly longer answer is required, usually containing two distinct points.]*

    (i)   The 'acre' represents Germany before unification, which both Austria and Prussia attempted to 'plough', or control. The result was 'dispute'.

(ii)   The Battle of Sadowa.

(iii)   The Treaty of Prague.

2. THE NATURE OF THE GERMAN CONSTITUTION SET UP IN 1871

Source F: from a speech by Benjamin Disraeli, leader of the Conservative Party, in the House of Commons, 9 February 1871.

This war represents the German revolution, a greater political event than the French revolution of the last century.

Source G: A criticism of the 1871 constitution by a political publicist, writing in 1875.

It is clear that a country containing as many different elements as Germany does, a country entwined with its neighbours on all sides and bordering on six different nationalities, a country, moreover, that has experienced a history comparable to no other in respect both of the variety of political forms created and the intrinsic importance of its events – that such a country must necessarily have achieved a constitution peculiar to itself. If this constitution was to be amended or improved, how could the appropriate forms be found except by deriving them from existing conditions? Instead an attempt was made to borrow these forms from various foreign constitutions and by means of such a compounded copy to produce a German national constitution, while at the same time proclaiming the principle of nationality which ought rather to have excluded anything foreign. What a strange contradiction!

Source H: from the writings and letters of the Prussian historian Heinrich von Treitschke.

(30 July 1866) There was a time when the ideas of French democracy dominated Germany and when those sudden and successful street battles in the capital city of a centralized state which decided the fate of a country served as models of glorious revolutions. The last decade has taught us that the great political upheavals of civilized peoples as a rule take place by other means, through the agency of orderly military forces ... The German revolution, too ... received its first impetus from above, from the Crown.

Source I: from a report by Bismarck to Wilhelm I, 29 March 1871.

The constitutional position of the Federal Council [Bundesrat] in the North German Confederation as well as in the German Empire derives its peculiar character from the fact that its members are bound by the instructions issued to them by their governments and therefore do not, like the deputies to the Reichstag, represent the whole but only the state which nominated them.

Source J: a letter from Bismarck to Bray (Prime Minister of Bavaria), 4 November 1870.

As to the basis of these negotiations, I should prefer the establishment of a close Confederation to any other. The basis is, in my view, the only one which meets the wishes of the German nation. It is the only one, therefore, suitable for the foundation of permanent institutions, while it is at the same time sufficient to assure such a position to Bavaria in the Germanic Confederation, to which on account of her importance, she has a claim.

Questions

1. (i) Explain the reference to 'This war' (Source F). (2 marks)
   (ii) Explain the meaning and purpose of the 'Reichstag' (Source I). (2 marks)
*2. In what ways do the arguments of Sources F, G and H differ? (4 marks)
3. What questions should a modern historian ask about the usefulness and reliability of Sources G and H? (5 marks)
4. What do Sources I and J show of Bismarck's concept of German unity? (4 marks)
5. Do Sources A to J, and your own knowledge, show that there had been a German revolution by the end of 1871? (8 marks)

Worked answer

*2. *[This type of question is more complex than the first. It needs a combination of argument and pin-point references to the specified sources. The word 'differ' needs to be covered in a way which includes all three sources. Quotations should be brief and integrated into your own sentences.]*

In Source F the term 'revolution' is used by Disraeli in a diplomatic sense, as affecting the balance of power in Europe. By contrast, the focus of Sources G and H are on internal change. There is, however, a fundamental difference between G and H. The political publicist (Source G) argues that Germany's political change was contradictory, since borrowing from 'various foreign constitutions' had conflicted with the 'principle of nationality' which should have 'excluded anything foreign'. Source H, by contrast, maintains that borrowing 'ideas of French democracy' had manifestly failed and that 'orderly military forces' were necessary for unification. Since the 'impetus' came 'from above', the inference is that this now excluded external influence from below.

2

DOMESTIC POLICIES, 1871–90

BACKGROUND NARRATIVE

Bismarck was Chancellor of the Reich between 1871 and 1890. He served under three Kaisers: Wilhelm I (1871–88), Friedrich III (1888) and Wilhelm II (1888–1918). In the process he took responsibility for Germany's domestic and foreign policies.

Several stages have been traditionally identified in Bismarck's domestic policies. During the early 1870s the process of German unification was completed by the implementation of a common currency and commercial regulations for all the German states, along with criminal and legal codes. This involved a close co-operation with members of the National Liberal Party who had always been enthusiastic advocates of German unity. In the same decade Bismarck took action to restrict the influence of the Catholic Church in a series of measures collectively known as the Kulturkampf ('culture struggle'). These brought him into direct conflict with the Centre Party. By 1879, however, Bismarck's priority was the introduction of tariffs to replace the previous policy of free trade. This produced a rift between Bismarck and the National Liberals and a reconciliation between Bismarck and the Centre. Also at the end of the 1870s, and for the rest of his administration, Bismarck took action against the Social Democrats, a party formed to represent the interests of the working class. He attempted to destroy the movement through repressive measures embodied in a series of anti-socialist laws. At the same time, he tried to outbid the SPD for the support of the workers by introducing insurance covering sickness, accident, old age and disability.

Bismarck's position depended ultimately on the Kaiser. Until 1888 he could rely on the support of Wilhelm I. But Friedrich III was far more progressive in his political sympathy. Even while he was Crown Prince, he had made it known that he opposed Bismarck's conservatism and repressive legislation. Bismarck therefore attempted to build up a position which would undermine Friedrich. In 1887, for example, he promoted an electoral alliance – the Kartell – between the National Liberals and the Prussian, Junker-based Conservative Party. This did well in the election but Bismarck's fears seemed to have been rendered groundless anyway by Friedrich's premature death after only four months on the throne. The third Kaiser, Wilhelm II, was more unpredictable. He too was suspicious of Bismarck's methods. This time Bismarck was unprepared: he failed to renew the Kartell and, when he fell out with Wilhelm in 1890 Bismarck found that he had no real support. His hasty attempts to build another alliance came too late to prevent the Kaiser's pressure for his resignation.

What was the role of Bismarck in these developments? Throughout the period 1871–90 he had to react quickly to events within Germany as they occurred. This meant that he was constantly having to adjust his tactics and switch his allies. At the same time, there were several underlying influences which seemed to propel Germany into a pattern of change which Bismarck could do comparatively little to resist. In the context of unification, he referred to his 'floating with the current' and 'steering'. The focus of Analysis 1 is the practical difficulties confronting Bismarck and the effectiveness, or otherwise, of the measures he took to deal with them: this is the 'steering'. Analysis 2 considers the underlying trends – or 'current' – which helped shape Bismarck's reaction and which limited his initiative.

ANALYSIS (1): WHY DID BISMARCK'S DOMESTIC POLICIES CHANGE BETWEEN 1871 AND 1890 – AND HOW SUCCESSFULLY WERE THEY IMPLEMENTED?

By one perspective, Bismarck was in control of his own political destiny and of that of Germany. The statesman who had done more than anyone else to create the Reich concentrated after 1871 on policies which would preserve it intact. The underlying dynamic was conservative and the initiative was taken by Bismarck himself. He resorted to a series of policies, some ingenious, some less so, in order to maintain and strengthen the status quo. At the same time, he was constrai e ' by the new constitution. There was a limit to what he could d., against the will of the Reichstag, which meant that he had to devise schemes to maintain its support or, at the least, to contain its opposit'on. Hence he adopted the role which he found instinctively distasteful – of manoeuvring between the political parties. He was, however, determined to avoid any permanent dependence on them. In his own words, he aimed to establish 'an understanding with the majority of the deputies that will not at the same time prejudice the future authority and governmental powers of the Crown or endanger the profic'ency of the army'. (1) Sometimes Bismarck was able to take the initia've. On other occasions he simply had to respond to events which occur ad' and try to bring his objectives into line with the new situation. This might mean having to abandon a policy which was clearly not working and pursue aims elsewhere.

Bismarck's initial priority was the internal consolidation of German unity. This meant tying up any loose ends through legislation and, at the same time, taking action to deal with any perceived threats to the new German state. To do this, he took measures which may, in retrospect, be seen as positive and negative, and as combining success with failure.

The positive – and largely successful – approach was to consolidate the fabric of unification. This involved close co-operation with the National Liberals, a party he disliked but which was useful to him on this occasion. The result was the flow of legislation through the Reichstag, organised by the National Liberal deputies Bamberger and Lasker, providing for a common currency and commercial code and unifying the civil and criminal codes of all the German states. With relatively little effort on his part, therefore, Bismarck was able to fill some of the gaps left in the 1871 Constitution. The cost was to his reputation with the Prussian-based Conservative Party, which was suspicious of his apparent flirtation with liberalism. The Conservatives, however, underestimated Bismarck's capacity for Realpolitik, or the ruthless subordination of means to objectives.

It soon became apparent that Bismarck's temporary collaboration with the National Liberals had another – and more negative – purpose. This was the campaign to undermine the position of the Catholic Church in Germany through the Kulturkampf, along with an offensive against the Catholic Centre Party in the Reichstag. Bismarck considered that the Catholic Church represented a dual threat to the new Reich. On the one hand the Bull of Papal Infallibility issued by Pope Pius IX, which was intended to reactivate the spiritual and temporal influence of Rome, might well make Catholicism an international power for the first time since the seventeenth century. This might also be used by Austria and France, two Catholic countries recently defeated by Prussia, to sow dissent within Germany through the Centre Party. Bismarck's concern about this possibility of separatism was all the more important since Catholics comprised 37 per cent of the population of Germany and included within their number ethnic minorities like the Poles of Posen and West Prussia and the French of Alsace and Lorraine.

The measures taken against the Church show Bismarck at his most manipulative. His own view was conservative and he relied upon Protestant influences on the Prussian and Reich governments to launch the initiative. Hence Falk's May Laws of 1873 and 1874 weakened the influence of the Church over education, introduced state inspection of all schools, made the appointment and training of priests a state responsibility, expelled the Jesuit order, and fully legalised civil procedures for marriage. Bismarck knew that this line would also be strongly supported by the National Liberals, who considered that the traditional authority of the Church had been a retarding factor in the evolution of a constitutional and progressive state. Their view was best expressed by the historian von Sybel, who said in 1874: 'We can see that if ever a state has rebelled against clerical pretensions from sheer necessity, from the duty of self-preservation, it is our state.' (2) Hence Bismarck was channelling two quite disparate influences: a Protestant–conservative attempt to cut down the possible challenge within the new Reich to Prussia's ascendancy; and a liberal initiative designed to prevent a traditionalist institution from impeding the growth of a new, predominantly secular, liberal German state. The result was a paradoxical combination of liberal and illiberal influences – the hallmark of so much of Bismarck's administration.

Bismarck was equally capable of shifting the political balance, reversing party alliances and diverting policies into new channels. This was particularly apparent at the end of the 1870s, when he reversed his allies and targets. Instead of depending on the National Liberals and confronting the Centre, he sought the support of the latter even if it meant alienating the former. There were several major reasons for this, all sudden and unexpected developments which Bismarck had somehow to accommodate.

The first was that the Kulturkampf was patently unsuccessful. German Catholics, especially in Bavaria and in the Polish areas of Prussia, hastened to support an encyclical issued by Pius IX in 1875 declaring the legislation on the Church invalid. In any case, Bismarck came to the conclusion that he had exaggerated the threat of separatism based on religion. There were other, more dangerous, ideological threats and it was now highly unlikely that France or Austria would be able to destabilise Germany by using Catholicism as a lever. The French Republic was also beginning to adopt an anticlerical policy, while diplomatic relations between Germany and Austria were moving towards an alliance. Instead, there were other problems. One had already been pursued in parallel to the Kulturkampf, but it now became necessary to concentrate more exclusively on it. A second was an economic priority which had to be addressed in 1879. Both needed a political realignment.

Various socialist groups had united in 1875 to form the Social Democratic Party (SPD), the programme of which called for a 'free state and socialist society', the 'elimination of all social and political inequality', improved working conditions in factories, and 'state supervision of factory workshop and domestic industry'. Bismarck was appalled by the long-term plan of the SPD to bring about a socialist state. This would subvert the 1871 Constitution, destroy the competitive power of German industry by imposing labour regulations, and threaten the national base by fostering an international conspiracy. Thus Bismarck launched a campaign against the SPD in which he openly defended ruthless measures: 'In dealing with Social Democracy the state must act in self-defence, and in self-defence one cannot be finnicky about the choice of means.' In fact, Bismarck attempted two very different methods which, at first sight, appear contradictory but which were clearly intended to be complementary. One was the anti-socialist campaign launched in the Anti-Socialist Law of October 1878. This allowed for the use of emergency powers for up to a year, prohibited socialist assemblies and fund collections and censored or banned socialist publications.

But, despite the banning of all but two socialist papers and the virtual elimination of trade unions, these measures were ineffectual. The

SPD used evasive tactics to sidestep the Anti-Socialist Law: they held secret conferences abroad and used bowling, gymnastic and cycling clubs as fronts for local organisations which maintained contacts with the party caucus in the Reichstag. Socialist ideas were also disseminated through a newspaper, the *Sozialdemokrat*, founded in Zurich in 1879. The result was that Bismarck was forced to make a further adjustment during the 1880s. This time he had to temper repression with a policy of 'state socialism', whereby he tried to outbid the Social Democrats for the support of the proletariat by means of state-sponsored legislation covering sickness insurance (1883), accident insurance (1884) and old-age and disability insurance (1889). It is true that these measures made Germany the most progressive of the major powers in its treatment of working conditions, but the regime did not receive the credit for which Bismarck had hoped. The advances were seen as the result of pressure exerted by the SPD – and could be expected to increase in line with further pressure in the future. Throughout the period of Bismarck's chancellorship, the electoral support for the SPD grew steadily – from 493,000 in 1877 to 550,000 in 1884 and 1,427,000 in 1890. By 1890, indeed, Bismarck had become so aware of the failure of his policy of state socialism that he reverted to one of repressive legislation, a move which brought him into direct confrontation with Kaiser Wilhelm II (see below).

Meanwhile, Bismarck was forced to come to terms with the effects of an economic depression which hit Germany and the rest of Europe from 1873 onwards. He was forced to heed the powerful pressures for tariffs exerted by the industrial and agricultural interests, both of which were fearful of being undercut by cheap imports. But, if he could not afford to ignore the demand for protection, Bismarck was also aware that he could reap some benefit from a change of economic policy. Strongly opposed in principle to instituting a national income tax, Bismarck welcomed the opportunity to increase revenues from indirect taxation since it would be easier to keep these out of the scope of Reichstag control. The snag was that the National Liberals, a traditionally laissez-faire party, were opposed in principle to instituting such a change. As it turned out, this did not matter. Bismarck was now ready to break his association with the National Liberals. This meant abandoning the main features of the Kulturkampf in order to win the support of the Centre Party under its leader Windthorst – but Bismarck seized the opportunity offered by the election of a new Pope in 1878 to improve relations with the Catholic Church. In 1879 this paid off when he was able to put together a bloc in the Reichstag of Conservatives, Free Conservatives and Centre deputies to push through protective tariffs against the opposition of the SPD and most of the National Liberals. In this way he was able to sidestep the possible humiliation of a shattered Kulturkampf and, in the words of one foreign observer, achieve 'one of the most substantial triumphs of his political career'.

The period 1878–79 therefore saw a major change of direction in which Bismarck abandoned his alignment with the National Liberals and gained instead the support of the Conservatives and Centre. The most tangible result of this was the introduction of tariff reform. The question now arising, however, was whether Bismarck would be able to maintain such a balance and keep his position through the next decade.

In some ways Bismarck's continuing twists and turns brought considerable success. For example, the National Liberals were never able to mount an effective challenge against him in revenge for the ruthless way in which he had used and then discarded them. Indeed, the party split: the more progressive element moved to the left to form the Freisinnige (Independent) Party in 1884, leaving the National Liberals as a rump to the right. Most of the latter actually came to support Bismarck on a regular basis – especially in the form of the Kartell – the electoral alliance between the National Liberals and the Conservatives of 1887. He also maintained his ascendancy over the Kaisers until 1888. With Wilhelm I he had taken the initiative at the outset and had retained it until the end of the reign in 1888. Concerned about the prospects of a liberal successor, he had taken every measure possible to neutralise the influence of Friedrich III (1888). In the process, he had built up the Kartell and created a military atmosphere in Germany by forcing an Army Bill through the Reichstag and deliberately intensifying colonial rivalries with Britain. As it turned out, Friedrich ruled for less than four months before dying of cancer.

On the other hand, there were clear instances of failure during this period. For example, the Kartell brought temporary security to Bismarck's position but he soon saw it as an encumbrance. The main problem was the constant friction between the National Liberals and the Conservatives, never the most natural political allies, in which Bismarck generally supported the latter. Hence he was increasingly inclined to try to bypass it and by 1889 it had withered as a result of his neglect. This meant that his political base was looking more precarious than at any time since the 1870s. The alternative, which was being actively considered by Bismarck, was to construct a new Kartell. This would involve creating a split within the Centre to match the one he had accomplished with the National Liberals: the result would be a permanent base of unassailable support in the Reichstag comprising the whole of the right wing of the political spectrum. The Centre was, however, more cohesive than the National Liberals and, under the effective leadership of Windthorst, held together in a determination to see the measures of the Kulturkampf properly rescinded – which Bismarck was prepared to do in his second 'Peace Bill' of 1887. The Centre was quite willing to lend its support on specific issues in the Reichstag in return for such concessions. But they were not prepared to undertake an unconditional alliance. Bismarck's attempt in 1890 to create a new Kartell between the Centre and Conservatives therefore failed. This came at a crucial time since Bismarck needed a strong base of support in the Reichstag to maintain his credibility with Kaiser Wilhelm II. Another failure is that, although Bismarck had out-manoeuvred Friedrich, he was confronted with the completely unknown quantity of Wilhelm II when Friedrich died suddenly. Bismarck found himself at loggerheads with the new monarch on virtually every issue. Wilhelm opposed the ending of the Kulturkampf, wanted to remove the measures against the SPD and was generally more sympathetic to the social problems of the working class. Bismarck hoped to force Wilhelm into compliance by another turn. He would construct a second Kartell based on the Conservatives and the Centre and fight an election based on the need to intensify anti-socialist legislation to contain the growing 'red peril'. For the first time, Bismarck found himself outmanoeuvred and isolated, as Windthorst refused to guarantee the support of the Centre, and the Kaiser found the confidence to 'drop the pilot' in 1890.

How successful was Bismarck overall? Each of the phases referred to involved a realignment of his relationship with the various political parties. As in the case of German unification, this can be seen as a deliberate policy of realignment to weather the various storms he encountered.

He showed some skill in this. He used the National Liberals to introduce measures to complete the process of unification and get through the legislative basis of the Kulturkampf. Then, when he switched his policy in 1879, he managed to cut the National Liberals down to size and yet still win them back into supporting the Kartell in 1887. He succeeded in getting the support of the Centre Party in 1879 for the switch to the policy of protection, even after his offensive of the Kulturkampf. He did manage to undermine the position of Friedrich III, although that unfortunate monarch died before being able to challenge Bismarck. He kept the support of the Conservatives throughout the period, even though they suspected some of his individual policies. And he delayed the emergence of the SPD as a mass parliamentary party. By the time of his resignation in 1890, it was nowhere near to being the largest party in the Reichstag – a position it was to attain in 1914.

Yet there were also failures. He had to acknowledge that the Kulturkampf was a miscalculation and legislation introduced in the 1880s reversed many of the original measures of the 1870s. He never succeeded in cutting the Centre Party down to size in the way he did the National Liberals – and eventually the Centre leader, Windthorst, had a direct hand in his fall from power. His anti-socialist policies did no more than delay the expansion of the SPD. And he was unable to consolidate his position in relation to the third Kaiser as he had, although in different ways, with the first and second. This showed, in the words of the novelist Fontane, that 'the power of the Hohenzollern monarchy ... was stronger than Bismarck's genius and his falsehoods'.

Questions

1. To what extent was Bismarck in control of Germany's domestic issues between 1871 and 1890?
2. Was Bismarck a 'ruthless' politician?

ANALYSIS (2): WHAT UNDERLYING INFLUENCES HELPED SHAPE GERMANY IN THE BISMARCK ERA?

Analysis 1 provided a view of Bismarck apparently making the decisions as to what policies should be introduced: sometimes he was able to take the initiative, sometimes he had to react to emergencies and unforeseen circumstances to try to regain the initiative and keep his position intact. This is all from the perspective of looking *down* upon Bismarck operating on the *surface* to control the political, social and economic structure of Germany.

But was this control real or apparent? Analysis 2 takes a different perspective. It looks *up* towards Bismarck from *below* the surface. Here two broad trends become evident. One affected the whole of industrialised Europe, including Germany. On top of this is another which relates more specifically to the German experience. Almost all the decisions apparently taken by Bismarck – in a frenzy of twisting and turning – can be explained logically as the influences coming to the surface from both levels. Analysis 2 therefore reduces the importance of the personal decisions attributed to Bismarck in Analysis 1.

The approach so far has been the way in which Bismarck responded to developments, seized opportunities and switched his policies. The focus has therefore been on decisions taken on the *surface* of the German political system. Increasingly, however, historians have concentrated their attention on the *underlying* trends in Germany's development. These produced the changes to which Bismarck had to respond, sometimes as opportunities to be exploited, sometimes as crises to be resolved. Throughout his chancellorship, Bismarck was never an entirely free agent and was always operating within real constraints. Although these must have appeared contradictory and confusing at the time, they appear more obvious in retrospect.

Two levels of underlying change can be identified. One affected the whole of industrialised Europe. The other was the more specific application of this to Germany. Looking from below at what Bismarck was doing on the surface can give a very different perspective of how much choice he actually had.

Mommsen and other recent German historians have laid considerable emphasis on the consistency of certain trends across the more advanced parts of Europe. The first was the spread of more representative government, of which the German Constitution of 1871 was only one example. Others included the new liberal state set up in Italy from 1861, the 1867 Reform Act in Britain, the Ausgleich (1867) in Austria-Hungary, and the Republican Laws in France (1871). The general movement, according to Mommsen, was dynamic and liberal, ensuring the end of the 'system of conservative monarchical states' of the period up to 1848. (3) Germany was therefore not alone in adapting a traditional power structure to more liberal principles. There were also attempts to extend the scope of reform: the 1870s saw the peak of liberal influence across Europe at the time that Bismarck was collaborating with the National Liberals in Germany.

Then came more turbulent times as everywhere moderate liberal influences were severely tested. In Germany the split within the National Liberal Party had its counterparts in the secession of the Liberal Unionists in Britain and the rift in France between the Opportunists and the Radicals. Meanwhile, a more specifically Continental trend was the emergence of mass parties aimed at particular parts of an enlarged electorate. These took two main forms: populism, which often had a religious emphasis; and socialism, which was directed at an ever expanding working class. In Germany the former was embodied in the Centre Party, the latter in the SPD. Elsewhere the same trend occurred in Belgium, the Netherlands and eventually in Italy, while socialism became particularly strong in France. This caused considerable problems of political adjustment, and Bismarck's tortuous twists and turns over the Kulturkampf were by no means unique. Nor were his subsequent reconciliation with the Centre and his attempts to mobilise populism on the side of conservatism and against socialism. This was very much the trend in Italy at the turn of the century.

This political turbulence was caused by economic changes which again affected much of industrialised Europe. Broadly, the late 1850s and 1860s had seen a rapid economic growth which had engendered massive confidence and had coincided with the importance of political liberalism. But this was followed, from 1873, by a prolonged depression, accompanied by a slowing production and a general fall in prices and wages. Agriculture was particularly affected but industry, too, began to feel the chill. All this cast doubt on the viability of the laissez-faire economic principles. Hence, there were powerful pressures for tariff reform, leading to the partial discrediting of political liberalism and the emergence of new political combinations. In Germany this process destroyed the liberals' political cohesion, moving some to the left and others to the right. Bismarck could therefore be seen to have gone with a general trend rather than inventing policies which were unique.

So there is a European dimension to economic and political change in the 1870s and 1880s. On top of this, we can see more exclusively German manifestations of these trends.

We should perhaps start with a second look at the process of and follow-up to unification. The traditional view is that unification had been accomplished by 1871 and that the next two decades consisted of attempts by Bismarck to maintain tight political control over the new institutions and structure. The emphasis is very much on preserving the status quo against threats to it from inside and outside Germany. There is, however, another possibility: instead of 1871 representing the end of movement and the beginning of consolidation, it might actually have been a stage in a longer process of change which reached its climax in 1879. The latter date produced a much clearer picture of what a united Germany actually meant – and of who was going to rule it. This is certainly the view of German historians such as Böhme. By this analysis, Bismarck was responding to an economic dynamic which helped change the circumstances of the early years of the Reich. Just as the boom of the 1850s and 1860s prepared the way for unification, so the depression of the 1870s and 1880s provided for a redefinition of who controlled this unity. This period saw the emergence of the socio-political combination of agrarian interest and industrial power which was the dual foundation of control over the Reich until 1914. Bismarck contributed to the process but certainly did not direct it.

In 1871 the logical inheritors of German unity appeared to be the National Liberals. Their laissez-faire economic theory had apparently been proved correct by the boom of the 1850s and 1860s and they had had a hand in the creation of the constitution of the North German Confederation which was, in turn, largely incorporated into that of the Second Reich. Given their buoyancy, did Bismarck actually have any choice other than to go along with them in the early 1870s, perhaps in an effort to control the pace of liberalisation? Then, with the onset of depression in 1873, which accelerated from 1875, the whole undercurrent began to change direction. There was a shift away from laissez-faire towards protectionism, and from progressive optimism to defensive conservatism.

The underlying impetus was economic, but the surface manifestations were social and political. The economic problems of overproduction, falling prices and foreign competition were, of course, dealt with by the introduction of tariffs in 1879. But the process involved a shift in the whole political direction taken by the Reich and the composition of the elite which really controlled it. Liberal optimism gave way from the mid-1870s to a crisis mentality in which enemies were manufactured – initially in the form of Catholic separatism, then more seriously as revolutionary socialism. This meant that Bismarck's Kulturkampf, the legislation against the SPD and the Tariff Law of 1879 were all part of a fundamental realignment which was redefining the scope of the new Germany. The key feature was the development of a political and social elite which joined together in defence against the perceived threats of Catholics and workers. This comprised the industrialists and the agriculturalists, all of whom were converted to the need for protection. Industrialists had tended to support either the Free Conservatives or the National Liberals, while the landed interests, especially the Junkers, provided the core of the Conservative Party. It is therefore hardly surprising that there should have been a wing of the National Liberals which was prepared to shoot off to the right and make new allies, or that Bismarck should have found it quite logical to think in terms of the Kartell of National Liberals, Conservatives and Free Conservatives. This all fits into what has been described as Sammlungspolitik, or the 'politics of pulling together'. This was no artificial alliance forged by Bismarck to prolong his career, but rather the emergence of an elite which was to dominate the rest of the period of the Second Reich.

One pattern appears to be at odds with all this. Why, if crisis was a necessary part of the creation of the Reich's elite, did Bismarck try to end it by seeking reconciliation with the Centre Party and the detachment of the working class from the SPD? There is a possible explanation. Crisis was necessary for the *formation* of Sammlungspolitik but not for its continuation: indeed, perpetual crisis is a contradiction in terms. Hence, Sammlungspolitik might be seen as embodying two stages. The first was the establishment of the industrial–agricultural–military elite. But the second was embedding this elite into Germany by whatever degree of acceptance could be won over. The elite needed this broader consent given that the German political system was a representative one. The Centre Party was an obvious target for reconciliation since it had as its natural constituency huge numbers of Catholics in Bavaria, West Prussia and the industrial Rhineland. This gives a certain logic to Bismarck's decision to end the Kulturkampf and, during the 1880s, to repeal earlier legislation and extend the range of the Kartell. The same tactic could hardly be applied to the SPD, since this was considered to be an inveterate enemy of the Reich. But why not try to win over the working population while at the same time starving the SPD of its support? This explains Bismarck's policy of social insurance and, perhaps, even his deliberate promotion of German imperialism in the late 1880s as a device to extend to the masses a feeling of patriotism.

All of these trends could be used to show that Bismarck was working within parameters which were not set by him. Or, to adapt his own metaphor, he was doing rather more 'floating' with the 'time stream' than 'steering' within it. This perspective reduces the dimensions of Bismarck's personal influence in the Second Reich, although we should avoid the extreme of allowing him no initiative at all. Cutting the Bismarck myth down to size also alters the perspective of the relationship between Bismarck's Germany (1871–90) and Wilhelmine Germany (1890–1914). Instead of being a radical departure from Bismarckian Germany, the underlying trends ensured that Wilhelmine Germany was really a continuation of it. This theme is explored in Chapter 4.

Questions

[These should be compared with the answers given to the same questions at the end of Analysis 1.]

1. To what extent was Bismarck in control of Germany's domestic issues between 1871 and 1890?
2. Was Bismarck a 'ruthless' politician?

SOURCES

1. THE POWER OF BISMARCK

Source A: an extract from Ludwig Bamberger's *Herr von Bismarck*, published in 1868.

Politics is not a science; at most it is an art. Consequently one of the greatest dangers to which one is exposed is that of falling into rigid traditional formulas.

Source B: an entry in the diary of Lieutenant-Colonel Bronsart von Schellendorff, chief of operations in the Prussian General Staff, 7 December 1870.

Count Bismarck is really beginning to be fit for a lunatic asylum. He has complained bitterly to the King that General Moltke has written to General Trochu and maintains that, being a negotiation with a foreign government, this should fall into his own sphere of competence. But General Moltke, as a spokesman of the High Command, has written to the Governor of Paris; the matter is therefore a purely military one ... The King, to whom General Moltke spoke about this matter, of course finds the whole thing very disagreeable.

Source C: from a speech by Bismarck to the Reichstag, 1881.

I have often acted hastily and without reflection, but when I had time to think I have always asked: what is useful, effective, right for my fatherland, for my dynasty – so long as I was merely in Prussia – and now for the German nation? I have never been doctrinaire ... liberal, reactionary, conservative – those I confess seem to me luxuries ... Give me a strong German state, and then ask me whether it should have more or less liberal furnishings, and you'll find that I answer: Yes, I've no fixed opinions, make proposals, and you won't meet any objections of principle from me. Many roads lead to Rome. Sometimes one must rule liberally, and sometimes dictatorially; there are no eternal rules ... My aim from the first moment of my public activity has been the creation and consolidation of Germany, and if you can show a single moment when I deviated from that magnetic needle, you may perhaps prove that I went wrong, but never that I lost sight of the national aim for a moment.

Source D: a description of Bismarck by Lady Emily Russell, wife of the British ambassador, 1880.

The *initiated* know that the emperor ... has allowed Prince Bismarck to have his own way in *everything*; and the great chancellor revels in the absolute power he has acquired and does as he pleases. He lives in the country and governs the German Empire without ever taking the trouble to consult the emperor about his plans, who only learns what is being done from the documents to which his signature is necessary, and which His Majesty signs without questions or hesitation. Never has a subject been granted so much irresponsible power from his sovereign, and never has a minister inspired a nation with more abject individual, as well as general, terror before. No wonder, then, that the crown prince should be so worried at a state of things which he has not more personal power or influence to remedy than anyone else in Prussia, whilst Prince Bismarck ... terrorises ... Germany with the emperor's tacit and cheerful consent.

Questions

*1. (i)   Of which political party (Source A) was Bamberger the leader? (1 mark)
     (ii) Who was the emperor referred to in Source D? (1 mark)
     (iii) What political position was occupied by Bismarck (a) at the time of Source B and (b) at the time of Source C? (2 marks)
2.   To what extent does Bismarck's assessment of himself in Source C conform to the characteristics described by Bamberger in Source A? (4 marks)
3.   Sources B and D are both highly critical of Bismarck. In what ways are they similar and how do they differ? (5 marks)
4.   Which of Sources A to D would, in your view, be the most useful to the historian studying Bismarck's political methods, and which would you consider the least useful? (5 marks)
5.   Using Sources A to D, and your own knowledge, discuss the view that Bismarck's main strengths as a politician were his moderation and adaptability. (7 marks)

Worked answer

*1. *[It is important to move through these questions as quickly as possible while, at the same time, being sufficiently precise to avoid losing any marks.]*

   (i)   The National Liberals.
   (ii) Wilhelm I.
   (iii) (a) Minister President of Prussia (b) Minister President of Prussia and Reich Chancellor.

2. BISMARCK AND THE KULTURKAMPF

Source E: from a speech by the King of Prussia to the Prussian Council of Ministers, 17 July 1871.

I have reservations ... about appointing as head of an institution for the training of future primary school teachers an adherent of the new dogma of the Catholic Church which manifests dubious consequences in its effect on the political situation.

Source F: from a speech by Bismarck in the upper chamber of the Prussian parliament, 10 March 1873.

The question before us is, in my opinion, distorted, and the light in which we see it is a false one if we regard it as a religious ecclesiastical question. It is essentially a political question. It is not, as our Catholic citizens are being persuaded, a matter of a struggle of a Protestant dynasty against the Catholic Church, it is not a matter of a struggle between belief and unbelief, it is a matter of the conflict, which is as old as the human race, between monarchy and priesthood ...

Here what is at issue is the establishment of two confessional states that would necessarily find themselves in a position of dualistic conflict, one of which would have as its sovereign ruler a foreign ecclesiastical prince whose seat is in Rome, a prince who because of the recent changes in the constitution of the Catholic Church is more powerful than it used to be. If this programme had been realised we would therefore have had, instead of the unitary Prussian state, instead of the German Empire which was in the course of development, two political organisms running in parallel: one with its general staff in the Centre Party, the other with its general staff in the government and person of His Majesty the Emperor. This situation was a totally unacceptable one for the government; and it was its duty to defend the state against this danger.

Source G: from a memorandum written by the Prussian Minister for Public Worship and Education, Heinrich von Mühler, to Bismarck, 14 October 1871.

I beg to submit to Your Highness in brief compass a programme of those legislative and administrative measures which are necessary in the field of education and ecclesiastical administration and in respect of which I desire energetic action.

I regard as of paramount importance a clarification of the relations between state and Church and emancipation of political and civil interests from subordination to the Church. This heading includes:

(1) Full freedom of secession from the Church and exemption for those who secede from duties and contributions to their former Church ...

(2) Regulation of civil matters, in particular with regard to civil marriage ... In principle I am in favour of civil marriage ...

(3) Abolition of supervision of schools by organs of the Church and unconditional subjection of schools to agencies of the state ...

(4) A decree requiring state censorship of pastoral letters and similar publications of Church authorities in so far as these concern political subjects ...

(5) Banning the Jesuit Order throughout Germany ...

Source H: The number of seats in the Reichstag held by the Centre Party between 1871 and 1890.

1871	63
1874	91
1877	93
1878	94
1881	100
1884	99
1887	98
1890	106

Questions

1. (i) What is being referred to in Source F by the words: 'because of the recent changes in the constitution of the Catholic Church is more powerful than it used to be'? (2 marks)

   (ii) Why was the 'Jesuit Order' (Source G) singled out for such radical treatment? (2 marks)

2. What, according to Sources E, F and G, was at issue in the Kulturkampf? (4 marks)

3. To what extent did the measures in Source G reflect the priorities shown in Sources E and F? (6 marks)

4. To what extent does Source H confirm that the Kulturkampf benefited the Centre Party? (5 marks)

*5. 'The Kulturkampf was a political conflict. When he realised that it would not work on a political level, Bismarck abandoned it.' Do the Sources, and your own knowledge, support this view? (8 marks)

Worked answer

5. [This question should produce the longest of the answers. About fifteen minutes should therefore be allocated to it in an examination. The emphasis should be on whether the 'Kulturkampf' was a 'political conflict', as shown in 'the Sources' and 'your own knowledge'. Furthermore, there needs to be discussion as to whether Bismarck did abandon the Kulturkampf when 'he realised it would not work on a political level'. All these must be covered and it is important to distinguish between 'the Sources' and 'your own knowledge'.]

Sources E and F support most strongly the view that the authorities regarded the Kulturkampf as a political conflict. Source E, however, relates more to the attitude of the King of Prussia, while Source F is a more explicit statement of Bismarck's policy. In it he maintained that it would be a distortion to see it as 'a religious ecclesiastical question'. Indeed, it was 'essentially a political question'. To this he added several major precedents for such a confrontation between Church and state. This was, in fact, a justification for the measures shown in Source G, which had been introduced two years earlier. Again, the focus was on the 'emancipation of political and civil interests from subordination to the Church' through regulations concerning education, marriage and censorship. But, although the political element was always foremost in his mind, Bismarck would have been strongly aware of the religious elements. Not shown in these sources is the importance on Catholic doctrine of the Bull on Papal Infallibility and the substantial concentration of Catholics in the south of Germany and in Prussia.

The Sources provide no direct reasons for abandoning the Kulturkampf, although one can be inferred from Source H. This shows that the popular support for the Centre Party, regarded by many as the political arm of the Catholic Church in Germany, held up very well from 1874 to 1881, increasing their seats in the Reichstag from 91 to 100. This would have shown Bismarck that there could be no easy political victory over the Catholic Church. There are, however, other influences behind Bismarck's change of policy, not shown in the Sources. One was both political and economic – the need for the support of the Centre Party for the introduction of tariff reform. The other was political and diplomatic – winning Germany over to a closer relationship with Austria. Both involved reconciliation between Church and state. It was not so much that Bismarck realised that he could not win the political conflict, but rather that his priorities had changed by 1879.

3

FOREIGN AND COLONIAL POLICIES, 1871–90

BACKGROUND NARRATIVE

In the decade leading to unification, Germany had been involved in three wars – with Denmark (1864), Austria (1866) and France (1870–71). For the rest of Bismarck's career Germany remained at peace, although the period saw hectic diplomatic activity in Europe and the beginning of imperial expansion overseas.

The main targets of Bismarck's diplomacy were Russia, Austria-Hungary and Italy. In 1872 he drew up the League of Three Emperors (Dreikaiserbund) with Russia and Austria. The terms were to maintain the status quo in Europe, co-operate in the elimination of socialism and work for peace. It was not a military alliance and it soon appeared highly vulnerable. The problem was that Austria and Russia became increasingly antagonistic over the situation in the Balkans. The trouble started when, in 1877, Russia went to war with Turkey in support of subject peoples like the Serbs and Bulgarians who had revolted against Turkish rule. Russia's victory over Turkey alarmed Austria, which increasingly feared for its own position in the area. Bismarck, therefore, brokered an international Congress at Berlin which revised the settlement inflicted on Turkey by Russia and attempted to satisfy the needs of the participating powers.

Within a year of the Congress of Berlin, Bismarck had drawn up a secret treaty – the Dual Alliance – between Germany and

Austria-Hungary. By this, the two countries undertook to assist each other if either was attacked by Russia: in the event of an invasion of one of them by a country apart from Russia, the other would remain neutral. In 1882 the Dual Alliance was extended into the Triple Alliance. By this, Germany, Italy and Austria undertook to support each other if any were attacked by two powers, although Italy explicitly excluded any possibility of war with Britain.

Meanwhile, Bismarck had revived the Dreikaiserbund in 1881. This committed each of the three powers to maintain a benevolent neutrality should any of them be involved in a war with a fourth. The agreement was renewed for a further three years in 1884. But the security this seemed to provide was ruined by another crisis in the Balkans between 1885 and 1887, this time in Bulgaria. Again, there was a prospect of conflict between Russia and Austria, in the event of which Bismarck attempted to safeguard Germany's position. In 1887, therefore, he drew up a secret Reinsurance Treaty with Russia, by which Germany and Russia agreed to remain neutral if either were attacked by a third power.

This was the last major agreement over which Bismarck presided before his resignation in 1890. During the following two decades a counter-alliance gradually developed. In 1893 France and Russia agreed to support each other in the event of a war involving either against two other powers, while Britain sorted out her colonial rivalries with France by the Entente of 1904 and with Russia by the 1907 Convention.

So far, the perspective has been confined to Europe. There was, however, also an expansion of German interest in Africa and the Pacific. In 1884 Germany raised the flag in South West Africa, Kamerun and Togo. This was followed in 1885 by German colonisation in German East Africa. By 1890, therefore, Bismarck bequeathed to Germany a network of alliances in Europe and a patchwork of colonies overseas.

These developments suggest two key questions. Why, and with what success, did Bismarck pursue his diplomatic policies in Europe? And why did Bismarck follow an expansionist policy beyond Europe?

ANALYSIS (1): WHY, AND WITH WHAT SUCCESS, DID BISMARCK PURSUE HIS DIPLOMATIC POLICIES IN EUROPE?

What is most surprising about the interpretation of Bismarck's foreign policy between 1871 and 1890 is not so much that it has attracted controversy, but rather that this controversy is far less wide ranging than with his domestic policy. Perhaps it is time to redress this. Overall, possible explanations for his apparently complex system of alliances and alignments can be grouped into two main categories. One has an external focus on diplomacy, while the other links foreign policy more directly with domestic issues. Each category, in turn, subdivides into Bismarck's role being either pivotal, the result of his own decisions, or more peripheral, with the real impact coming from external influences.

The diplomatic explanation for Bismarck's foreign policy is the one advanced by most historians and followed by most students. According to this approach, Bismarck undertook a role after 1871 which was fundamentally different to that before. Whereas he had previously contributed to the unification of Germany by disrupting Europe, his priority was now to prevent any *further* change and to maintain the international status quo as established in 1871. This meant that he was content with Germany's frontiers as they were and was not intending to seek further expansion. He did not wish to absorb the German part of Austria-Hungary, preferring to accept the existence of two German-speaking powers in Europe working in close co-operation with each other. This relationship would safeguard Germany in the future, whereas further expansion would only stretch and weaken Germany's base.

Objectively, there were two main threats to the status quo. One was the recovery of France to its former military strength, which might lead to a war of revenge against Germany for the recovery of Alsace-Lorraine. The other was a collision between Austria and Russia in the Balkans which could leave Russia moving towards an alliance with France. Bismarck was convinced that it was in Germany's best interests that both of these should be prevented. The priorities were therefore to keep France in isolation, to prevent Russia from feeling the need to end that isolation, and to construct a secure diplomatic network for the protection of Germany. By 1890 all this seemed to have been achieved. France was still alone in Europe, while Germany had military agreements with Austria in the Dual Alliance (1879) and with Italy as a result of the Triple Alliance of 1882. Russia, meanwhile, had been kept in association with Germany by the Dreikaiserbunds of

1873, 1881 and 1884 and, when these finally gave way, by the secret Reinsurance Treaty of 1887.

But was Bismarck personally responsible for all this? The traditional 'diplomatic' view is that he was. According to Langer, 'No other states-man of standing had ever before shown the same great moderation and sound political sense of the possible and the desirable.' (1) This view is certainly supportable. Throughout his period as Chancellor, Bismarck had seized opportunities and reacted to crises to steer Germany to security – while, at the same time, helping to maintain peace in Europe. Everything he did fits into a logical pattern and has a convincing reason. From the outset he deliberately isolated France and courted Russia, the two powers most likely to upset the status quo. His Dreikaiserbund of 1873 was an attempt to revive the traditional co-operation between Russia, Austria and Prussia that was prevalent in the period 1815–54. When this was threatened between 1875 and 1878 by the Balkans, Bismarck sought to provide a lasting overall settlement at the Congress of Berlin (1878). Concerned, however, about the possibility of a future clash between Austria and Russia, he drew up the Dual Alliance in 1879. This had a double purpose: to enable Germany to restrain Austria from provoking Russia in the future and, should that fail, to have Austrian support in the event of a Russian attack on Germany. He went further: anticipating that Russia and France might still form an agreement, he extended the Dual Alliance to Italy to form the Triple Alliance (1882). His reasoning here was that Germany should always seek to be part of a larger combination: 'when there are five [powers], try to be à trois'. (2) These measures were, however, precautionary: he did not intend to lose his influence over Russia. Hence in 1881, and again in 1884, he brought Russia back into the Dreikaiserbund. This was disrupted by the Bulgarian Crisis of 1885, which snapped any remaining bond between Russia and Austria and posed the threat of Russia's gravitation towards France. The Reinsurance Treaty of 1887 was Bismarck's solution. In strict secrecy, this guaranteed Germany's support for Russian interests in Bulgaria and Germany's neutrality in the event of an Austrian attack on Russia. Technically, this did not infringe the Dual Alliance, since Germany had undertaken to support Austria only in the event of aggression by Russia. The real advantage of the Reinsurance Treaty to Bismarck was that Russia would remain neutral in the event of any war between Germany and France, provided that France were the aggressor. Thus, by 1890, Bismarck had carefully and systematically put together a system of alliances and alignments which, properly used and maintained, would serve the related purposes of keeping Europe at peace and maintaining Germany's position of predominance. Unfortunately, all this was upset by the blunders of his successors. The failure in 1890 to renew the Reinsurance Treaty started the reverse momentum which led eventually to the Franco-Russian alliance of 1894. In the longer term, it must be admitted, Bismarck's 'system' proved too complex for lesser statesmen to maintain. Criticism of him, therefore, centres not on his failure but rather on his being too clever by half.

The alternative 'diplomatic' approach is that Bismarck simply reacted to events, with no preconceptions and certainly with no overall scheme. As with his involvement in the unification of Germany, any appearance of calculation was retrospective, part of the myth built up by Bismarck in the reminiscences he wrote in retirement. The other powers provided him with his opportunities: all he had to do was to manipulate these at short notice. Sometimes he overreacted and had to compensate later in the form of other changes. This case has been put most strongly by A.J.P. Taylor, who maintained that Bismarck 'lived in the moment and responded to its challenge'. It is possible to compile evidence for this more careless and impulsive Bismarck. It was he who had insisted on the annexation of Alsace-Lorraine by the Treaty of Frankfurt (1871), thereby setting up the original problem of French revanchism. Perhaps the Dreikaiserbund of 1873 reduced the risk of war with France by removing Russia from the equation. But it was actually Tsar Alexander II who had suggested Russia's membership: Bismarck merely accepted the opportunity. The Dual Alliance (1879) was certainly a response to the Balkans Crisis but, as Taylor argues, Bismarck rushed into it. He was also manipulated by Austria, to the extent that he said to the Austrian Foreign Minister, Andrássy: 'If you will not accept my terms, then I am forced to accept yours.' (3) These gave more security to Austria than to Germany. Bismarck then tried to compensate for his action in two ways. One was the renewal of the Dreikaiserbund (1881) in an attempt to prevent the situation where a war between Austria and Russia would have to involve Germany on the side of Austria. The other was to secure the southern border of a vulnerable ally by forming the Triple Alliance (1882): the inclusion of Italy was intended as much to prevent Italy from attacking Austria as to help Germany in any war between Germany and France. When all these rather hasty arrangements were threatened by the Bulgarian Crisis, Bismarck took a high risk with his secret bilateral agreement with Russia in 1887. The Reinsurance Treaty could easily have wrecked the Dual Alliance, which is why Bismarck's successors failed to renew it. By 1890 Bismarck had, it is true, kept France and Russia apart. But this was more by luck than judgement. Far from inheriting and then destroying a successful system, the next Chancellor, Caprivi, found that the system was already on the point of collapse. Policies after 1890 were merely an acknowledgement of this. What was needed was a new approach, one which would be more dynamic and establish a more lasting basis for German security and power.

These two 'diplomatic' views are therefore fundamentally opposed. They do, however, have in common the emphasis on *external* influence on Bismarck's policies. It is strange that, given the trends of interpretation for other periods of German history, more has not been made of the connection between Bismarck's foreign and *domestic* policies. The underlying point is that the two should not be seen as separate parts of the Chancellor's decision making, but rather as integral. As with the 'diplomatic' approach, however, the 'domestic' connection has two very different applications.

The first possibility is that Bismarck consciously brought domestic and foreign policies into harmony and directed them in parallel. In the years immediately following unification, Bismarck pursued a policy of loose co-operation to convert unification into a more stable form. Hence, in domestic policy he aligned himself with the work of the National Liberals in completing the unification of German institutions and legal codes. In foreign policy his preference was for a loose agreement with Austria-Hungary and Russia, through the Dreikaiserbund, to strengthen Germany's position in Europe through the maintenance of generally harmonious relations. The principle behind both was one largely of laissez-faire within a favourable overall climate. Then came a general change of approach, the abandonment of laissez-faire in a move towards protection both at home and abroad – focused on the year 1879. In the case of domestic policy it involved abandoning the attack on the Catholics through the Kulturkampf, while in foreign policy there was a link up with Catholic Austria. At home there were renewed arrangements with traditionalists and attempts to create political combinations; abroad, the equivalent was the renewed Dreikaiserbunds. In both cases there was a target to keep isolated. Internally, it was the progressive and socialist influences, whether in the form of a liberal Kaiser or a dangerous revolutionary threat like the Social Democrats, either of which might upset the internal balance of the Reich. Externally the threat was France, which was both republican and revanchist. Up to the time of his resignation in 1890, Bismarck had therefore followed a policy of even more stunning complexity than has been previously acknowledged. He operated not one system but two – and kept them in parallel with each other. Wilhelm I once acknowledged that Bismarck contrived a juggling act with six balls while on horseback. We might increase the balls to ten and have him standing astride two horses. It is hardly surprising that his successors could not continue the act. Towards the end of his career Bismarck was frustrated by a Kaiser who could not see the value of what he was trying to do either at home or abroad. Wilhelm II thought he was exaggerating the threat of the SPD and so refused to renew the Anti-socialist Laws. He also failed to see the threat of an alliance between Russia and France and saw no need to renew the Reinsurance Treaty. In both cases, as Bismarck pointed out, the result was the turn of the tide in favour of the Social Democrats and of France in the 1890s.

The connection between domestic and foreign policy can therefore be used to elevate Bismarck's reputation. Alternatively, it can cut him even further down to size. There was a much more haphazard inter-action between events and influences at home and abroad and Bismarck found himself less and less in control and more and more beleaguered. He constantly had to struggle to pull one into line with the direction taken by the other, without it being really apparent what was causing it to take that direction. In other words, Bismarck was at the mercy of forces which he could not fully understand, let alone manipulate. For example, the 1870s saw co-operation with the National Liberals within Germany, which was strangely at odds with the apparent recreation of the old combination of autocratic powers abroad in the form of the Dreikaiserbund. There was perhaps more logic behind the simultaneous ending of the Kulturkampf at home and the Austro-German alliance abroad. Which, however, influenced the other? Did Bismarck abandon the Kulturkampf in his search for an alliance with Austria? Or did the alliance make sense once he had decided to end the Kulturkampf? As for the apparent balance between domestic and foreign policy in the 1880s, Bismarck was, in reality, pulled in different directions. He wanted to reduce the chance of war between Austria and Russia and yet had to emphasise that chance in order to put an Army Bill through the Reichstag in 1887. He tried to reconcile the two by taking practical steps in the Reinsurance Treaty to reduce the threat of war, knowing full well that if he lost the connection with Austria as a result, he would also forfeit any possibility of support from the Centre Party. And this was the grouping that he was actually trying to engage in the construction of a new Kartell in 1890. In these circumstances Bismarck found his position more and more tenuous. Perhaps this shows that he had actually lost the connection between domestic and foreign issues and that it was his successors who pulled them back into line through a more powerful underlying logic of the type examined in Chapter 4.

Questions

1. How fully was Bismarck in control of Germany's foreign policy between 1871 and 1890?
2. Were there any connections between Germany's foreign policy and domestic issues between 1871 and 1890?

ANALYSIS 2: WHAT WAS BISMARCK'S ATTITUDE TO COLONIES AND WHY DID GERMANY ACQUIRE AN OVERSEAS EMPIRE DURING HIS CHANCELLORSHIP?

Bismarck's attitude appears, to say the least, inconsistent. Before 1885 he showed comparatively little interest in German overseas expansion, seeing colonies as an expensive luxury akin to 'a poverty stricken Polish nobleman providing himself with silks and sables when he needed shirts'. (4) Then came an apparent burst of enthusiasm as Bismarck declared German ownership of part of New Guinea and groups of Pacific Islands, as well as four coastal areas in Africa: Togoland, Kamerun, South West Africa and East Africa. Finally, he appeared to lose interest, having gone through what Mommsen refers to as a 'mere passing phase'. In 1889 he referred to 'German colonial humbug', while he informed a surprised Reichstag in 1890: 'I am not a colonial man.' (5) He refused to sanction the expansion of German East Africa beyond the island of Zanzibar and a narrow coastal strip, and was certainly strongly opposed to the possible annexation of Uganda in 1890.

The overall pattern therefore showed initial indifference, followed by a burst of enthusiasm which, in turn, gave way to renewed indifference. Not surprisingly, a range of theories can be advanced to explain this.

The most obvious is that the acquisition of colonies was a natural corollary to the process of German unification. Other European powers had become involved in a renewed round of imperialism during the 1870s after a good half-century of inactivity. France was expanding her role in North Africa; Britain was undergoing a similar conversion under Disraeli. Why should Germany be the exception? Townsend considers that Bismarck intended to enter the colonial field as soon as he had the chance and his establishment of consuls in Africa in the 1870s was a sign of 'his cautious preparation and watchful waiting'. (6) The impetus he needed was subsequently provided by the growth of national enthusiasm for colonies, which was channelled by organisations like the Kolonialverein, an association which specifically pressed for the foundation of a German overseas empire. By the mid-1880s, Bismarck had come to the conclusion that the time was right and that he could safely abandon his initial caution. In any case, such caution was by no means unique to Germany. Disraeli, for example, had once referred to 'our wretched colonies' as 'millstones around our necks' (7); the same man later made Empire one of the three pillars of Conservative Party policy. Bismarck was, therefore, even if belatedly, part of a broader process of conversion. In part this was due to Germany's later maturation as a nation state. But by the 1880s there were strong internal economic pressures for new markets and materials, while nationalist groups sought fulfilment through imperial expansion. A similar momentum drove Italy into the search for an overseas empire less than a decade after the completion of her own unification in 1870. Logical or not, the process was for both countries as inexorable as the westward expansion of the United States. As for the slowing momentum after 1887, this was quite possibly due to the growing costs of administration – to the need to follow acceleration by the brake. Again, this was not unique to Germany.

Fitting the German experience into a broader pattern does tend to reduce the personal importance of Bismarck in the process. Not all historians would go along with this. There has always been a strong case for Bismarck using colonial issues as a means of securing European objectives: colonial policy was in this respect an integral part of his foreign policy. Thomson, for example, maintains that 'The naked power politics of the new colonialism were the projection, on to an overseas screen, of the inter-state frictions and rivalries of Europe.' (8) Fieldhouse agrees: 'imperialism may be seen as the extension into the periphery of the political struggle of Europe'. (9) The leading figure in this process was Bismarck. Even Berghahn, who has brought extensive revision to other periods of German history, maintains that 'Bismarck was guided by soberly pragmatic reasons', and that he was using colonial issues as 'part of an attempted reorientation of German diplomacy'. (10)

How does this argument work? Briefly, Bismarck was essentially a Continental statesman and had no love of colonies for their own sake. Nevertheless, he saw the usefulness of using Africa as a means of diverting energies and tensions away from Europe. Throughout his chancellorship he was concerned above all with the possibility of French revanchism for the loss of Alsace-Lorraine. Bismarck therefore took every opportunity to drive a wedge between France and any potential allies by encouraging imperial rivalries between them. He was fully aware of the importance of imperialism as a means of restoring prestige; as Gambetta had said, 'In Africa, France will take the first faltering steps of the convalescent.' (11) There were several instances of Bismarck's encouragement of French expansion for European motives. In the first place, he secretly incited France to take Tunisia in 1878. This so antagonised Italy that the latter eventually joined the Triple Alliance in 1882, accepting the obligation to assist Germany in the event of an attack by France. Second, Bismarck worked on deliberately creating tension between France and Britain. He did this to divert French attention from Alsace-Lorraine with the promise of German support for France against Britain in Africa. Hence, he upheld French claims in Egypt, despite British concerns about the security of the Suez Canal. He also co-operated with France during the Berlin Conference between 1884 and 1885 over the issue of the Congo. He told the French Ambassador in 1885: 'Renounce the question of the Rhine; I will help you in securing all the satisfaction you require on all other points.' (12) To show his good faith Bismarck deliberately sought to antagonise Britain by challenging British interests. The most direct way of doing this was by annexing territory adjacent to existing British colonies. Togo was next to the Gold Coast, Kamerun to Nigeria, South West Africa to the Cape, and German East Africa to British East Africa. Hence, according to A.J.P. Taylor, German colonies were the 'accidental by-product of an abortive Franco-German entente'. (13) Other historians agree with this theory. According to Williamson, much as Britain disliked Bismarck's policy, she 'had no choice but to tolerate it'. (14)

All this has a certain logic. Britain was too heavily involved in protecting more important interests in Egypt against French and Islamic threats (and the Indian subcontinent against the prospect of Russian expansion) to register too much concern about German claims to the remnants of Africa. Hence the Anglo-German Agreement of 1886 recognised German claims in East Africa. Bismarck, therefore, found himself with an empire as a reward for his diplomatic pressure – whether he actually wanted this or not. When he found that the German East Africa Company was unable to provide an effective administration, shortly followed by the failure of the South West Africa Company, Bismarck lost any remaining enthusiasm for colonies. This was particularly the case when, in 1887, the imperial pressure on Britain failed to produce an alliance with her and it was no longer quite so important to keep on good terms with France since the Reinsurance Treaty of 1887 guaranteed Russian neutrality should France attack Germany. There is an additional component here. Eyck argues that colonies would be a useful bargaining tool for Germany to use if things became too difficult with Russia. Bismarck could trade off German colonies in exchange for British support. Again, however, 1887 proved to be a turning point in that Britain turned down the prospect of an alliance, while Russia signed the Reinsurance Treaty. Since Bismarck no longer had any need to think in terms of a trade-off, the colonies had lost their diplomatic significance.

By this approach, the strengthening and weakening of Bismarck's interest can be related directly to the ebb and flow of priorities in his European diplomacy. There is, of course, an alternative. The origins of German colonies can be sought in domestic influences and pressures.

In one way the domestic interpretation is merely an inversion of the diplomatic interpretation, the projection of overseas rivalries on to the domestic screen. Several historians explicitly acknowledge this as a possibility, including Taylor and Berghahn, the latter referring to the 'domestic and electoral calculations' in Bismarck's colonial policy. (15) There is one particular example of this, to which Bismarck himself later admitted. Bismarck's domestic security centred on the support of the Kaiser. Although he could be certain of the goodwill of Wilhelm I, he had the strongest reason to suspect the hostility of Crown Prince Friedrich, who was liberal and pro-British in his views. Bismarck feared that, once he came to the throne, Friedrich would insist on setting up a cabinet on British lines. In his attempt to discredit the British system, Bismarck deliberately engineered a policy of confrontation with Britain in Africa. According to his son, Herbert, Bismarck believed that 'we had to embark on a colonial policy' because it could be 'conveniently adapted to bring us into conflict with England at any given moment' (16).

A more direct domestic impetus was economic. German imperialism might well have been a search for markets and outlets for investment abroad. As soon as this became apparent, Bismarck started with the extension of consular facilities. As commercial involvement expanded, he moved quite logically to the principle of company rule – until he realised that the German government itself would have to take a share of the administrative costs. But the economic link may have been overstated. There was a limit to which colonies could actually absorb German investment which, in any case, was more likely to move in the direction of more developed areas like Latin America. Possibly more convincing is the search for an outlet for raw materials, but even this is a more significant factor in the 1890s.

Another 'domestic' explanation to the origins of German imperialism provides a more social slant, with the emphasis on the externalising of aggression as a means of diverting attacks on Germany's ruling elites. Wehler and others have argued that imperialism was a means of channelling the energies of the ever increasing proletariat into patriotism by stimulating interest in events abroad. There may well be something to this. A sense of political belonging to the new Reich could be created to counterbalance the feeling of social alienation within it. Patriotism, properly channelled, was the best antidote to social discontent and revolutionary activism. Imperialism therefore became closely integrated with conservatism – a dynamic force to re-invigorate the status quo. We could add to this Eley's view that colonial expansion was really the step beyond Sammlungspolitik – the further safeguarding of the elites which had defensively joined together in 1879. On the other hand, this all sounds a little contrived as a primary explanation. Is there a difference in principle between externalising social pressures and projecting diplomatic rivalries on to an overseas screen? Is there not, in both, the implication that imperialism was a tactical means of achieving an underlying objective which was not actually related to it? Can imperialism really be seen as a response entirely to other pressures, with no momentum of its own?

Perhaps: most historians seem to think so. But it makes sense to take a more integrated approach. For once, a genuine synthesis of all the arguments is possible. Germany was part of a general European phenomenon with an alternating stop–go attitude to imperialism. Bismarck, like Disraeli, found that imperialism was a useful means of rallying popular support, which the emerging elites in Germany desperately needed, while, at the same time, satisfying certain economic needs. Similarly, Bismarck was able to integrate specific components of his imperial policy into his foreign policy, just as the latter usually related fairly closely to his domestic objectives. But the convergence of these trends was neither sudden nor contrived. Nor were they exclusive of each other. Many of Bismarck's individual proposals and solutions may well have been ingenious, but it would be far-fetched to deduce from them individually an entire and deliberately created system. Again, it seems that Bismarck tried to steer with the current. In this, historians of Bismarck's imperialism have tried to indicate the direction he took. They have more successfully shown what was driving him.

Questions

1. Why did Bismarck change his mind about acquiring colonies for Germany?

2. How was Germany's colonial policy related to (a) her foreign policy and (b) her domestic policy?

SOURCES

1. BISMARCK'S ALLIANCES

Source A: from the Dual Alliance of 1879.

Article I. Should, contrary to their hope, and against the loyal desire of the two High Contracting Parties, one of the two Empires be attacked by Russia, the High Contracting Parties are bound to come to the assistance one of the other with the whole war strength of the Empires, and accordingly only to conclude peace together and upon mutual agreement.

Article II. Should one of the High Contracting Parties be attacked by another Power, the other High Contracting Party binds itself hereby, not only not to support the aggressor against its high Ally, but to observe at least a benevolent neutrality towards its fellow Contracting Party.

Should, however, the attacking party in such a case be supported by Russia, either by an active co-operation or by military measures which constitute a menace to the Party attacked, then the obligation stipulated in Article I of this Treaty, for reciprocal assistance with the whole fighting force, becomes equally operative, and the conduct of the war by the two High Contracting Parties shall in this case also be in common until the conclusion of a common peace.

Source B: from the Reinsurance Treaty of 1887.

Article 1. In case one of the High Contracting Parties should find itself at war with a third great Power, the other would maintain a benevolent neutrality towards it, and would devote its efforts to the localisation of the conflict. This provision would not apply to a war against Austria or France in case this war should result from an attack directed against one of these latter two Powers by one of the High Contracting Parties.

Source C: an extract from a private letter from Bismarck to the British Prime Minister, Lord Salisbury, 22 November 1887.

Given this state of affairs we must regard as permanent the danger that our peace will be disturbed by France and Russia. Our policy therefore will necessarily tend to secure what alliances we can in view of the possibility of having to fight our two powerful neighbours simultaneously. If the alliance between friendly powers threatened by the same belligerent nations were not forthcoming our situation in a war on both fronts would not be a matter for despair; but war against France and Russia allied ... would always be a sufficiently great calamity for our country for us to try and avoid it by an amicable arrangement with Russia, if we had to do it without an ally ... Thus we shall avoid a Russian war as long as this is compatible with our honour and security, and as long as the independence of Austria-Hungary, whose existence as a great power is of paramount importance to us, is not called into question.

Questions

1. (i) Apart from Germany, which was the other High Contracting Party referred to in Source A and Source B. (2 marks)
   (ii) Explain the meaning of the term 'reinsurance' (Source B). (2 marks)
*2. To what extent are the terms of the Reinsurance Treaty (Source B) compatible with those of the Dual Alliance (Source A)? (6 marks)
3. What questions should the historian ask about Source C as evidence for the motives behind Bismarck's relations with the other Great Powers? (5 marks)
4. 'Bismarck was prepared to go to any measure to prevent the risk of an alliance between Russia and France, even if this measure meant endangering relations with Austria-Hungary.' Using Sources A to C, and your own knowledge, say whether you agree with this view. (10 marks)

Worked answer

*2. [This question involves a careful comparison between the two sources, with a legalistic eye for possible conflicting details. Bearing in mind that the treaties were drawn up at Bismarck's instigation, there are unlikely to be any, but legality could be expected to sail close to the diplomatic wind. The answer should focus on precise references to the sources and, where relevant, to explanatory background knowledge.]

The Reinsurance Treaty did not, by a legal interpretation, conflict with the Austro-German Alliance. It undertook that Germany and Russia would observe a 'benevolent neutrality' if either 'should find itself at war with a third great Power'. The Austro-German Alliance had undertaken mutual assistance should 'one of the two Empires be attacked by Russia'. The Reinsurance Treaty explicitly excluded 'an attack directed against' Austria by Russia, or against France by Germany. Hence the Reinsurance Treaty did not conflict with the defensive emphasis of the Dual Alliance.

On the other hand, the difference between defensive and offensive wars must be open to interpretation. Should war have broken out between Austria and Russia, both combatants would have claimed to be acting defensively. In this case, the Reinsurance Treaty would have been invoked by Russia and the Austro-German Treaty by Austria. In this situation, legality would have had to succumb to diplomacy or expediency. Germany, in other words, would have had the choice between fighting Russia and not supporting Austria.

2. BISMARCK'S ATTITUDE TO OVERSEAS COLONIES

Source D: a report, relayed to London, of a conversation between Bismarck and the British Ambassador in Berlin, 1871.

He neither desired colonies or fleets for Germany. Colonies in his opinion would only be a cause of weakness, because colonies could only be defended by powerful fleets, and Germany's geographical position did not necessitate her development into a first class maritime power. A fleet was sufficient for Germany that could cope with fleets like those of Austria, Egypt, Holland, and perhaps Italy, scarcely with that of Russia, but it could not be a German interest so long as she had no colonies to rivalise with maritime powers like England, America, or France. Many colonies had been offered to him; he had rejected them and wished only for coaling stations acquired by treaty from other nations.

Source E: an extract from the memoirs of Chlodwig zu Hohenlohe-Schillingsfürst, adviser and future Chancellor. These were published in 1907.

In the evening of 22 February 1880 I had dinner with Bismarck ... At table we drank much port and Hungarian wine. Afterwards I sat with the Chancellor and spoke of many things. The Chancellor refuses all talk of colonies. He says that we haven't an adequate fleet to protect them, and our bureaucracy is not skilful enough to direct the government of such territories. The Chancellor also alluded to my report for the French plans for Morocco, and thought we could only rejoice if France annexed it. She would then be very occupied, and we could let her expand in Africa as compensation for the loss of Alsace-Lorraine.

Source F: Bismarck to the French Ambassador in 1885.

Renounce the question of the Rhine; I will help you in securing all the satisfaction you require on all other points.

Source G: a report of Bismarck's speech to the Budget Commission of the Reichstag, 23 June 1884.

If it were asked what means the German Reich possessed for protecting German undertakings in far-off places, the answer first and foremost would be the desire and interest of other powers to preserve friendly relations with her. If in foreign countries they recognised the firm resolve of the German nation to protect every German . . . it would not cost much effort to afford this protection. But of course if other countries were to see us disunited, then we should accomplish nothing and it would be better to give up the idea of overseas expansion.

Source H: from the memoirs of Herbert Bismarck, son of the Chancellor.

When we started colonies we had to face a long reign by the crown prince . . . and therefore had to launch a colonial policy in order to provoke conflicts with England at any moment.

Questions

1. Explain the references to 'the loss of Alsace-Lorraine' (Source E) and 'the crown prince'. (Source H). (2 marks)
2. What are the grounds shown in Sources D and E for Bismarck's early opposition to Germany acquiring overseas colonies? (4 marks)
3. Which, in your opinion, is the more reliable of Sources D and E for the historian studying Bismarck's attitude to German colonies? (5 marks)
*4. Why might Bismarck want to 'provoke conflicts with Britain at any moment' (Source H)? How much credence should be given to this Source? (6 marks)
5. Using Sources D to H, and your own knowledge, discuss the view that 'Bismarck's colonial policies were inconsistent'. (8 marks)

Worked answer

*4. [This question is in two parts. The first depends on a degree of outside knowledge to supplement the source, while the focus of the *second part is the nature of the source itself as historical evidence. Both parts must be fully covered.]*

There are two reasons why Bismarck might wish to 'provoke conflicts with Britain'. First, he was encouraging France to become actively involved in imperialism in Africa in order to divert her attention from the loss of Alsace-Lorraine; since France's main rival was likely to be Britain, disagreement with the latter would be proof of Germany's goodwill to France. Second, Bismarck feared that the accession of the Crown Prince Friedrich would lead to more constitutional government in Germany, since Friedrich admired the British system. If Bismarck could engineer a disagreement with Britain, the Crown Prince would be outmanoeuvred.

Source H has advantages and disadvantages as an interpretation of Bismarck's motives. Its main strength is the insight given by a member of Bismarck's family who would have been conversant with his ideas and methods. On the other hand, the memoirs were published some time after the event and may well have been embellished to put a more favourable construction on events; there may even have been an attempt to show his father as a politician of calculation and discernment.

4

DOMESTIC POLICIES, 1890–1914

BACKGROUND NARRATIVE

There was an almost complete change in the personnel responsible for domestic policy after 1890. Kaiser Wilhelm II (r. 1888–1918) assumed more direct control on the resignation of Bismarck. He was a diverse character, prone to a variety of personal complexes and inconsistent decisions. He was closely advised by officials who had no sympathy with the methods of Bismarck, initially Holstein, later Eulenburg and Tirpitz. The actual policies were carried out by the four Chancellors of the period. These were Caprivi (1890–94), Chlodwig zu Hohenlohe-Schillingsfürst (1894–1900), Bülow (1900–09) and Bethmann Hollweg (1909–17).

At first it seemed that Germany would become more progressive as, in 1890, Kaiser Wilhelm refused to allow Bismarck to reactivate earlier anti-socialist legislation, thereby precipitating the latter's resignation. After becoming Chancellor in 1890, Caprivi introduced his 'New Course', a policy aimed at social reform and commercial agreements with other countries to reduce tariffs. All he succeeded in doing, however, was to alienate the agricultural and industrial interests, without winning over the SPD. In 1894, therefore, the Kaiser replaced Caprivi with Hohenlohe. He was, however, merely a temporary appointment, designed to win back the support of the Centre Party and the Conservatives.

The promotion of Bülow to the chancellorship in 1900 was confirmation that the Kaiser was giving priority to foreign policy.

Bülow sought to divert opposition within the Reichstag through a more assertive policy abroad, but he was still obliged to take note of the opposition within the Reichstag and therefore to form blocs to keep his government afloat. This involved concessions both to the working class and to landed interests and industrialists. Bülow's administration also saw two major domestic crises. The first was the public outcry over the treatment of the Herero Uprising in the German colony of South West Africa in 1906; the Centre Party and the SPD challenged the government's record on colonial administration and publicised a series of atrocities. The second was the *Daily Telegraph* Affair of 1908, when the Kaiser alleged that only he stood between the German people and war with Britain. Bülow resigned over the issue in an attempt to secure the Kaiser's consent to a reduction in the spontaneous exercise of the royal prerogative.

Bethmann Hollweg, appointed as Bülow's successor in 1909, was even more than his predecessors caught up in the demands of foreign policy as Germany drifted towards war. His administration saw another major crisis. In the Zabern Affair (1913), the German army mistreated the civilian inhabitants of a town in Alsace and were subsequently not properly disciplined. Once it became clear that a breach of discipline had occurred in Zabern, the Kaiser, as commander-in-chief, ordered the transfer of the commanding officers rather than their court martial. This was tantamount to declaring that military interests were above the law. With the emergence of the SPD as the largest party in the Reichstag in the 1912 elections, it seemed that the ruling elites and the lower levels of society had become more antagonistic than ever. As it happened, however, the outbreak of war in 1914 provided a temporary reconciliation between them.

The two Analyses in this chapter focus on two very different issues. The first is a theme to which historians have recently given particular emphasis – the meaning and nature of the power structure in Wilhelmine Germany. The second is the more conventional question as to what those in power actually achieved.

ANALYSIS (1): WHO WAS IN CONTROL OF GERMANY BETWEEN 1890 AND 1914?

Until the 1960s this question would have been seen as a tautology: control was – or was not – exerted by those in control, meaning the administration in general and the Kaiser in particular. Following the influence of Fischer, however, a new wave of German historiography questioned the importance traditionally ascribed to individuals and, instead, placed the emphasis increasingly on the structure of German society and the tensions between its various components: these periodically found their outlets through the policies pursued by the representatives of the elites who controlled the government. Hence there is now a perceived dichotomy between the 'individualist' and 'structuralist' approaches. There is also a division between those historians who consider that power was exerted from above, whether by individuals or by structural elites, and those who oppose the 'top-down' interpretation with a 'bottom-up' alternative, which gives far more influence to the lower orders within society: instead of being simply manipulated, these contributed directly to the sort of pressures which eventually surfaced in the form of specific policies.

The traditional view is that there was a reversal of roles in 1890. Up to that point the Kaiser had been in theory the head of state and commander-in-chief of the armed forces. However, it was the Chancellor who had actually ruled Germany. Wilhelm I had been content to allow Bismarck to assume considerable discretionary powers, while Friedrich III had been too ill to make any change to this. From 1890, however, Wilhelm II reactivated the powers of the Kaiser with the clear intention of making the Chancellors play a subordinate role. Hence 'Bismarckian' Germany gave way to the 'Wilhelmine' era.

The expression of Wilhelm II's power was certainly more extensive as, unlike his two predecessors, he was determined to rule as well as to reign. He saw himself in a traditional Prussian role and was firmly convinced of the importance of divine right: he was on the throne 'by the grace of God'. His position in relation to his Chancellors was quite different to that of Wilhelm I to Bismarck. The 1871 Constitution gave him supreme control over the executive, the power of appointment and dismissal of all ministers. This he used on many occasions, not least in forcing the resignation of Bismarck in 1890. He also systematically undermined the position of Bismarck's successors, Caprivi (1890–94) and Hohenlohe (1894–1900) by accepting the advice of Holstein, originally a strong critic of Bismarck, and Tirpitz, Secretary to the Navy in 1897. As Chancellor, only Bülow (1900–09) was able to exert any real influence, and even he was forced to resign over his clash with the Kaiser concerning the *Daily Telegraph* Affair (1908). As King of Prussia, Wilhelm's authority was even more extensive, based as it was on the largely unreformed Constitution of 1851.

Wilhelm II underpinned this political authority in two ways. First, he established a very close link between the political administration and the army. Most of the government departments developed parallel military channels of decision making and communication. The extent to which he was prepared to uphold and defend the military can be seen in the Zabern Crisis of 1913, in which he refused to take any action against a number of German soldiers who had taken violent measures against the civilians of a town in Alsace. He was prepared, in the process, to defy a vote of censure by a large majority of the deputies and parties within the Reichstag. Second, Wilhelm controlled the development of public opinion; according to Mommsen all that he ever really wanted to do was 'to gratify public opinion . . . and, in particular, win the plaudits of the middle class and the intelligentsia'. (1) The government made extensive use of propaganda to help to shape this, especially during Bülow's chancellorship, when a complete overhaul was undertaken of the relevant machinery. He ensured that press offices were placed in each ministry to provide a favourable slant on any news which was issued. Certain newspapers with wide circulations were selected to present the government case: examples included *Norddeutsche Allgemeine Zeitung*.

By this analysis, therefore, power lay with the Kaiser. This did not, however, mean that it was effectively used. The basic problem was that the devious but carefully controlled policies of Bismarck gave way to the more haphazard and unpredictable approach of Wilhelm II. The result is often seen as chaotic. Germany was run by a man who has been variously described as eccentric, narcissistic or verging on the insane. The power which the Kaiser possessed was often used negatively: it turned in upon itself and created a vacuum, even, according to some historians, a political anarchy. Wilhelm made arbitrary appointments to compensate for his personal inadequacies and to bolster his distorted ego. According to Röhl (2) the Wilhelmine period was an exercise in irrational authoritarianism, a view which has its origins in the writing of the historian Quidde who, in 1894, indirectly accused Wilhelm of 'Caesarian madness'. (3) Examples of this included the obsession he showed for changing the uniforms worn by the German army and the notorious *Daily Telegraph* Affair, in which Wilhelm maintained that the German people were profoundly anti-pathetic towards Britain and that he was the only restraining influence upon them. This provoked almost unanimous condemnation from the Reichstag and an unsuccessful attempt to create constitutional constraints on the irresponsible exercise of his power.

This 'pathological' approach to historical analysis does not, however, provide a total explanation for the politics and policies of the period. Pulzer, for one, points to its shortcomings: 'it is difficult to accept his undoubted eccentricities as the alibi for the political mistakes of the Wilhelmine period, for no man, however powerful, can act alone'. (4) Placing the focus on the Kaiser devalues the contributions made by Caprivi to the development and implementation of the New Course, or of the Interior Minister Posadowsky to the extension of welfare legislation between 1900 and 1908. It also underemphasises the capacity of the Kaiser to make rational decisions, as he clearly did when rejecting Bismarck's attempts in 1890 to renew earlier legislation against the activities of the Social Democrats. Above all, the focus on an incompetent individual does not allow for the broader influences and pressures being exerted within Germany, of which most government policies can be seen as manifestations.

Since the 1960s there has been an alternative explanation to that of power residing with the Kaiser. Instead, Germany was dominated by a combination of social and economic forces which helped to shape both domestic and foreign policies. The emphasis is therefore on the structure of Germany rather than on the role of individual German leaders. Structuralism can, in turn, be seen from two different perspectives: these are generally called 'top-down' and 'bottom-up'.

The 'top-down' approach to structuralism focuses on the German elites and is largely the result of the work of Fischer (5) in the 1960s as refined by Wehler in the 1970s. (6) The latter is especially clear about the inadequacy of the 'individualist' approach, maintaining that '"Wilhelminism" is a term often used quite inappropriately to sum up this era.' The reason is that 'It was not Wilhelm II who imposed his will on government policy during this period, but the traditional oligarchies in conjunction with the anonymous forces of an authoritarian polycracy.' (7) These included the traditional landowning elites, the new industrialists, the officer corps and the diplomats. They attempted, through a process of rallying together, or Sammlungspolitik, to prevent the economic developments, then taking place in Germany, from leading to social levelling and political democratisation. Those in authority clearly reflected these aims. The Kaiser and his Chancellors, along with the advisers and military leaders, were all pursuing policies which would avoid the need for the elites to share power with the ever broadening layer of the working and lower middle classes. The result was a close link between domestic and foreign policies. The former aimed to prevent democratisation, by whatever means possible, the latter to divert the consequent pressures into a patriotic outlet in the form of 'social imperialism'. Within this overall pattern the individual policies of the Kaiser and his government were bound to vary and we should not look for total consistency. But this does not mean that they were directionless. On the contrary, the New Course and the reforms of Posadowsky were attempts to keep social change to a minimum through a policy of damage limitation; they were, in any case, offset periodically by the revival of more coercive measures. Whether or not the Kaiser committed individual blunders hardly affects the overall hypothesis that he was acting not as an individual but rather as the representative of a broader trend. He was the outlet for power, not the power itself.

This approach has extended in range and depth the study of domestic issues, and it can be applied to other societies in Europe. But there are critics of Wehler's structuralist 'top-down' analysis. The reverse method is the 'bottom-up', which has been applied largely by British historians and emanates from an interest and involvement in local history. Their new approach to Germany coincides with an extensive re-evaluation of English history as well, especially in the Tudor and Stuart periods.

Briefly, the argument of Evans, Blackbourn and Eley is that the ordinary people in Germany were not simply being operated as puppets by their masters, as the 'top-down' historians strongly imply. Rather, those groups who were excluded from the elites exerted a vital pressure on the development of policy. They comprised those who, according to Retallack, were beyond the 'barriers of geography, nationality, class, culture, religion and . . . gender'. (8) These 'out' groups generated their own radical pressures which forced responses from the elites, often against their will. One variant might be the beginning of mass fascism through what Evans describes as the 'political self-mobilisation of the petty-bourgeoisie'. (9) This clearly contributed to the growth of a more active foreign policy and is an example of the government responding to grass-roots pressures. In this respect, the authorities reacted to changes in public opinion rather than deliberately initiating that change. There has also been a sharp rejection of the notion that the workers were passive groups which could be manipulated from above. Their very concentration was bound to create its own pressure, especially in the Ruhr cities of Oberhausen, Dortmund, Duisburg, Hattingen and Recklinghausen, which contained 395,000 miners alone. The population of Bochum rose by 200 per cent between 1880 and 1910 compared with 44 per cent in Germany as a whole. The lower middle and working classes overlapped into the sectarian divide: many were also Catholic, with further reasons to pressurise the regime for concessions.

Such pressure could be exerted increasingly effectively through two parties which held the key to the functioning of the Reichstag after 1890 – the SPD and the Centre. The former was throughout the period a constant barrier to government policy which had to be overcome if legislation was to go through. This meant that the government had to court the Centre Party, without whose support it was impossible to put together a working majority. The Centre, as has been shown by Blackbourn, was rapidly losing its clerical character and was becoming very much a party led by lawyers and supported by the smaller bourgeoisie, especially in southern Germany. (10) Hence the working and lower middle classes were far from being politically neutralised by the establishment. Instead, they helped shape the way in which the government assembled its majorities which, in turn, influenced its legislation. It seems, therefore, that 'bottom-up' infiltration could have been at least a partial counterfoil to 'top-down' manipulation.

All of these views do not necessarily exclude each other. The most recent interpretations seem to be moving towards an overall synthesis. This might be attempted as follows: Bismarck continued, in his absence, to exert a residual influence after 1890 because of the direction which his policies had taken within the institutions he had set up. His successors made decisions as to what policies should be followed, whether in continuation of those of Bismarck or in opposition to them. To a considerable extent these were directly influenced by the needs of the elites from whom those in political authority were drawn. At the same time, the system which they tried to preserve was being gradually altered from the grass roots by increasing influences from the proletariat and also from the middle classes. These helped shape public opinion, of which the government became ever more conscious, and, in a narrower sense, confined the government's range of policy by their extensive representation in the Reichstag. How effectively the government responded is the theme of Analysis 2.

Questions

1. Which is the more convincing explanation of the exercise of power in Wilhelmine Germany: the 'individualist' or the 'structuralist'?
2. How influential were ordinary people in the power structure of Wilhelmine Germany?

ANALYSIS (2): HOW MUCH DID THE WILHELMINE GOVERNMENTS BETWEEN 1890 AND 1914 ACHIEVE IN THE DOMESTIC SPHERE?

The criteria for achievement in the domestic sphere may be said to include the overall efficiency of government, the effective handling of the Reichstag and legislation, the extent of reform, the strengthening of the economy, the maintenance of defence without upsetting other sectors, and a positive response to unexpected crises.

A fully effective administration required two conditions. One was the co-operation between the Chancellor, embodying actual executive power, and the Kaiser, as head of state. This had, on the whole, been the relationship between Bismarck and Kaiser Wilhelm I between 1871 and 1888. The other was a working agreement between the Chancellor and the Reichstag. Again, Bismarck had managed to secure this by creating political blocs to gain majority support on specific issues. After 1888 and, more noticeably, after Bismarck's resignation in 1890 the Chancellor became less and less the pivot that the 1871 Constitution had intended him to be. What now happened was that the Kaiser exerted more personal power and the Reichstag became more assertive in its criticism of government policy. The result was that the Chancellors were often caught between the two. It was not just that they were less adept than Bismarck at maintaining the domestic balance: they rarely got the chance to do so.

None of the Chancellors after 1890 had Bismarck's ability to keep the threads of government in his hands. Caprivi (1890–94) was a military man with little experience of political administration. There was always a strong suspicion that he was tightly controlled by the Kaiser and his clique of advisers. One of these, Eulenburg, fed the Kaiser's predilection for personal authority. The result was the dismissal of Caprivi, the one Chancellor with a genuine aptitude for the job. Hohenlohe (1894–1900), too, was under the influence of the Kaiser's retinue, especially Bülow (then Foreign Minister), Holstein and Tirpitz, whose main focus was to externalise domestic pressures. This may or may not have been a calculated move – or the response to growing demands from the elites. Certainly, Hohenlohe had little direct influence and his preference for administrative procrastination saw a further subordination of domestic interests to foreign policy. Bülow (1900–09) should, in theory, have been able to exert more direct influence since he had been one of the Kaiser's advisers in Hohenlohe's administration. As a landowner he also had the necessary connection with the elites. Yet, as Chancellor, his priority was always with foreign policy and he gave domestic issues his attention only when forced to do so by crisis. Bethmann Hollweg (1909–17) was more inclined towards administration than either Hohenlohe or Bülow and has been seen by most historians as being more concerned to try to balance different parties and interests. His administration was, however, blighted by the growing crisis in international relations which culminated in the outbreak of war in 1914.

The Chancellors also had some difficulty in managing the Reichstag after 1890. This was a potentially fraught area since the two mass parties nearly always held the balance there. The Centre Party, for example, ranged from a high of 106 seats in 1890 to a low of 91 in 1914 – a remarkable degree of consistency, while the SPD grew from 35 in 1890 to 110 in 1912. Successive governments had to rely on the support of the right-wing parties (the Conservatives, Free Conservatives and National Liberals) and usually needed the compliance of the Centre to ensure that they had a majority over parties likely to oppose their policies such as the Progressives, the SPD and the various national groupings. Normally the government succeeded in holding this support – but always at the cost of trimming its proposed legislation. The only time that the government could free itself from the Centre was between 1907 and 1909 when the result of the 1907 Reichstag election gave the combined parties of the right an overall majority, thus making possible the formation of the Bülow bloc. But even this collapsed in 1909 on the issue of inheritance tax, proposed by the government as part of a measure to finance the increase in battleships. Bülow resigned over the issue and the Centre Party had to be enticed into the new Blue-Black Bloc to secure the passage of the measure. It might, of course, be argued that their response to such difficulties shows that the Chancellors were successful in handling the Reichstag. But this amounted to little more than crisis management – certainly by contrast with the British system, where cobbling together disparate majorities for specific items of legislation was the exception rather than the rule.

A key factor in assessing the record of any government is the introduction of social reform. Certainly attempts were made to come to terms with the problems resulting from rapid industrialisation. As part of the New Course, legislation was introduced in 1890 placing limits on the employment of women and children in factories, while Sundays became a mandatory day of rest. The following year saw the introduction of a more refined system of industrial arbitration between employers and employees. Similar measures were introduced, during the chancellorship of Bülow, by the Minister of the Interior, Posadowsky. Accident insurance and pensions were made more widely available in 1900, the length of time over which sickness benefits could be paid was doubled in 1903, while in 1901 industrial courts were made mandatory and in 1908 further conditions were applied to child employment.

From one point of view such reforms were ahead of those of Britain. Indeed, there were elements within the British Liberal government from 1905 who were pro-German, not for reasons of foreign policy, but for the extent of Germany's social legislation. Against this, however, it could be argued that the motives for the reforms in Germany were diversionary and defensive; they were a tactical alternative to coercive measures, which were also used periodically. For example, between the reforms of Caprivi and Bülow came Hohenlohe's attempt to re-introduce Bismarck's legislation against socialism. When, however, the Reichstag resisted these measures, the Kaiser's government had to abandon repression and focus instead on renewed reform. This amounted to conciliation which was, at the same time, associated with the development of the policy of Weltpolitik as a means of making the working class more patriotic. The reforms in Britain were, by contrast, the result of a fundamental change in the perception of the role of the government in promoting the welfare of the people.

How effectively did the government control the economy? The economic component of Caprivi's New Course seemed to make considerable sense: he introduced a series of commercial treaties removing or reducing tariff barriers with Austria-Hungary, Italy, Russia and some of the Balkan states. These provided an outlet for German industrial exports while, at the same time, reducing the cost of food imports. They were, however, deeply resented by the landowners who now had to compete on harsher terms. Hence, they established the Agrarian League to press for their interests. The government's response seems to spell inconsistency. When the commercial treaties expired in 1902 Bülow's chancellorship failed to renew them and, instead, reimposed agricultural tariffs. To conciliate the industrialists, who now had no such protection, the tariffs had to be pitched at a lower level than the agrarians wanted, while the working class, faced with rising food prices, were conciliated by another round of social reform. Each stage in the process seems to indicate the lack of any underlying policy and, instead, a reaction to problems as they arose. There is, of course, an alternative explanation that the administration was taking a much broader and more subtle view, using economic issues alongside the promotion of Weltpolitik to create the sort of inner harmony which Germany badly needed. Kehr (11), for example, associates the tariff laws with the increases in naval expenditure. Both, it is sometimes believed, were intended to rally the upper and middle classes, while the working class was to be bought off with the prospect of social reforms and stirred up by patriotism. As it stands, however, this interpretation attributes a great deal of foresight and forethought which can be challenged on the grounds either of lack of documentary evidence for such a scheme or of its being unlikely, given the unpredictable and volatile personal influence of the Kaiser and his advisers.

One of the government's main priorities was to maintain and finance a high level of defence. This meant increasing Germany's military infrastructure to enable it to play a world role. This met with mixed success – it was less obvious with the army than with the navy. Any increase in the size of the army involved a struggle between the government and the Reichstag. The government itself was put under further pressure by the leading military personnel of the day; the Chief of Staff, von Schlieffen, demanded the enlargement of the army by 84,000. Caprivi, however, had enormous difficulties getting this through the Reichstag and had to make concessions in return, the most important of which was to allow a review of military expenditure on a five-yearly basis instead of every seven years as before. The creation and expansion of the navy proved a more popular project. The Navy Laws of 1897, 1900 and 1906 were less difficult to push through the Reichstag, largely because of the support given by the Centre Party. As a whole, the German population showed greater enthusiasm for the navy than for the army, probably because it was seen to transcend the narrow Prussian base and to provide a more genuine example of *German* power. The real problems of naval expansion appeared in Germany's foreign policy rather than at home. The enlargement of the navy forced an alienated Britain into agreement with Germany's Continental enemies, while the limitations on the army gave the General Staff a sense of urgency in dealing with France and Russia, both of which were catching up quickly from 1912.

A form of pressure which confronts every government is unpredictable crises. How well did the Wilhelmine regime handle these? The answer in each case was ambivalent, with the government making its point but doing very little to resolve the problem which had caused each crisis in the first place. Cracks appearing in the administrative structure were simply papered over. The first was in the colonial administration in South West Africa, over which Berlin appeared to have lost effective control. Following the 1906 Herero Uprising, the Centre and SPD challenged the government's policy after reports from Catholic missionaries of German maladministration and brutality in the colony. Bülow secured the dissolution of the Reichstag and a majority in 1907 for the Conservatives, and other parties of the right, over the Centre and SPD. On the other hand, few changes were made to the administration, giving the Allies the justification they needed to deprive Germany of all its colonies under the Treaty of Versailles in 1919. A second crisis, the 1908 *Daily Telegraph* Affair, showed the extent to which the central administration was being distorted by unconventional and unconstitutional use of the Kaiser's power. This was picked up by the Reichstag, which was forceful in its criticism – but no changes were made to the Kaiser's powers. Again, the government survived but no lesson was learned. The third crisis, the Zabern Incident of 1913, provides a similar example of damage limitation rather than a stimulus for more fundamental reform.

Between 1890 and 1914 Germany experienced a mixture of sound government, with periodic reform, and political insecurity leading to domestic policies which were less carefully considered. There appears to have been a chronological movement from one to the other. The major attempts at domestic change were the initial ones of Caprivi's New Course. Then, during Hohenlohe's chancellorship, the focus was switched to foreign policy, in the form of Weltpolitik. The effect of this was the relegation of domestic issues to the point that they became increasingly reactive – and therefore inconsistent. Historians have long argued the case for domestic pressures influencing the course of foreign policy. There is now scope for an investigation of the effects of foreign policy on the course of domestic policy.

Questions

1. What were the motives for domestic reforms in the period 1890–1914?
2. Which Chancellor achieved most in the domestic sector between 1890 and 1914?

SOURCES

1. MODERATION AND RADICALISM IN GERMAN POLITICS 1890–1914

Source A: from the *New York Herald*, quoting the words of the Centre Party leader, Windthorst, in March 1890.

In the new Reichstag new groups must be formed. The Centre Party will enter no permanent coalition, only such temporary combinations as may be necessary from time to time ... There can be no question of a systematic opposition on our part against the government ... The main thing is that everyone, without regard for party viewpoints, should unite in support of society and the government and protect them against attack.

Source B: an extract from the periodical *Die Nation*, 1894.

A government that wishes to capture people's minds and spirits must possess initiative. It must undertake reforms. And there is always need for great reforms ... A statesman who conducts a positive policy will always win a significant following, and a statesman who conducts an intelligent policy will always find this following among intelligent people. It is not enough for the government to reveal its immediate objectives from time to time; it must also reveal the long-term objectives toward which it is striving. It must not appeal solely to sober reason but must also understand how to appeal to the heart ... If today there still existed among us a party such as the National Liberal Party was during the first half of the seventies, in such a party the Reich Chancellor would find his natural support.

Source C: a coded telegram from the Kaiser to Caprivi on an interview with the King of Saxony, 8 September 1894.

I was pleased to see how clear the king was on the political situation and that his opinions fully agreed with mine ... He declared emphatically that if the Reichstag refuses repeatedly to accept measures for the protection of society it has forfeited its right to exist.

Source D: the view of the left-wing leader of the SPD, August Bebel, 1903.

I want to remain the deadly enemy of this bourgeois society and this political order in order to undermine it in its conditions of existence and, if I can, to eliminate it entirely.

Source E: the view of the moderate leader of the SPD, Eduard Bernstein, 1899.

Constitutional legislation works more slowly. Its path is usually that of compromise ... But it is stronger than the revolution scheme where prejudice and the limited horizon of the great mass of the people appear as a hindrance to social progress, and it offers greater advantages where it is the question of the creation of permanent economic arrangements capable of lasting ... In legislation intellect dominates over emotion in quiet times; during a revolution emotion dominates over intellect.

Questions

1. (i)   Who was Caprivi (Source C)? (1 mark)
    (ii) What type of socialism would have been advocated by the author of Source D? (1 mark)
    (iii) What term is usually given to the moderate wing of the SPD under Bernstein? (1 mark)
2. What might the government of the day have found in Sources A and B (a) a message of comfort and (b) a potential threat? (5 marks)
*3. What do Sources C and D have in common? (3 marks)
4. What are the main differences between the two types of socialism in Sources D and E? How does the use of language emphasise these differences? (6 marks)
5. 'During the period 1890–1914 Germany's domestic situation was dominated by moderate rather than extremist political views.' Using Sources A to E, and your own knowledge, say whether you agree with this view. (8 marks)

Worked answer

*3. *[At first sight, this might appear to be a mistake, since the contents of Sources C and D seem to have nothing in common. A further look, however, shows a similarity in the impatience shown by both Sources with the existing political system. This needs to be the focus of the answer. A single paragraph should suffice for the 3 marks available.]*

Although they come from the opposite ends of the political spectrum, Sources C and D both show dissatisfaction with the existing political situation – the Kaiser with an obstructive Reichstag and Bebel with 'bourgeois society and this political order'. Both see a solution in radical action. The Kaiser is considering the possibility of eliminating the Reichstag, Bebel of eliminating bourgeois society. Hence Source C shows the threat of a revolution from above, Source D of a revolution from below. Given the political situation between 1890 and 1914, neither was particularly realistic.

2. THE CHARACTER AND POWER OF KAISER WILHELM II

Source F: from an editorial in *Die Badische Presse* (4 October 1889) after a visit to the area from the Kaiser.

For the first time one can appreciate completely the significance of the greatest statesman of the last century, Prince Bismarck, that the youthful Reich now has the good fortune to have a Kaiser who wants to be his own chancellor. The wholesome influence that an active and vigorous monarchy can exert on the German Reich has not yet been fully realized in that the great Kaiser Wilhelm I was already aged, and his noble son Friedrich was already infirm. Kaiser Wilhelm II, however, with his youth and energy is 'the right man in the right place' for the new phase in the development of the Reich.

Source G: from a speech made by the Kaiser to recruits in the German army (18 April 1891).

The soldier and the army, not Parliamentary majorities and decisions, have welded the German Empire together. I put my trust in the army.

Source H: from a letter (dated 1900) by Prince Philipp zu Eulenburg to Bernhard von Bülow, later Chancellor. The letter refers to the Kaiser.

HM is no longer in control of himself when He is seized by rage. I regard the situation as highly dangerous and am at a loss to know what to do . . . These things cut me to the quick. I have had so much faith in the Kaiser's abilities – and in the passage of time! – Now both have failed, and one sees a person suffering whom one loves dearly but cannot help.

Source I: a description of the Kaiser by Maximilian Harden, editor of *Die Zukunft*, 1900.

All the important political decisions of the past twelve years have been made by him. Changes in trade policy, the build-up of the fleet, the belief in the German Reich achieving Weltmacht [world power] on an enormous scale, the friendly relations and secret treaties with England, the military campaign in China, all that and a lot more besides is his work. His objectives have been correct almost without exception but his chosen ways and means have been unfortunate.

Source J: Friedrich Naumann, a Lutheran pastor and politician, on the Kaiser's power, 1900.

In present-day Germany there is no stronger force than the Kaiser. The very complaints of the anti-Kaiser democrats about the growth of personal absolutism are the best proof of this fact, for these complaints are not pure invention but are based on the repeated observation that all policy, foreign and internal, stems from the will and word of the Kaiser. No monarch of absolutist times ever had so much real power as the Kaiser has today. He does not achieve everything he wants, but it is still more than anybody would have believed possible in the middle of the last century.

Source K: an interpretation of the Kaiser by Sigmund Freud, 1932.

It is usual for mothers whom Fate has presented with a child who is sickly or otherwise at a disadvantage to try to compensate him for his unfair handicap by a super-abundance of love. In the instance before us, the proud mother behaved otherwise; she withdrew her love from the child on account of his infirmity. When he had grown up into a man of great power, he proved unambiguously by his actions that he had never forgiven his mother.

Source L: an extract from a modern German historian, H.-U. Wehler.

It was not Wilhelm II who impressed his stamp on Reich policy but the traditional oligarchies in conjunction with the anonymous forces of the authoritarian polycracy. Their power sufficed even without a semi-dictator [Bismarck], although with the help of a Bonapartist strategy, to defend the citadel of power – however fatal the consequences.

Questions

1. (i) In Source G, the Kaiser was probably quoting a speech made by a former Minister President of Prussia in 1862. Name the person who made that speech and briefly explain the occasion on which it was made. (3 marks)
   (ii) Give an example of a physical infirmity suffered by Kaiser Wilhelm II and referred to in Source K. (1 mark)
2. What can be inferred from Source G about the Kaiser's own view of his political power? (4 marks)
3. Compare and contrast the views of the Kaiser given in Sources F, H, I and J. (6 marks)
4. How much credence should historians give to the view of Sigmund Freud about the Kaiser in Source K? (3 marks)
*5. To what extent do Sources F to K, and your own knowledge, support the view given by Source L on the personal importance of Kaiser Wilhelm II? (8 marks)

Worked answer

*5. [Most final questions will be on primary sources only and will involve seeking some sort of balance between them. This particular question involves a secondary source (L) which disagrees fundamentally with the line taken in the other sources. Additional knowledge is therefore particularly important for an overall balance.]

Wehler's central argument in Source L is that the Kaiser was not the crucial influence behind the policies of the Second Reich. This is not borne out in the other sources. Source J puts the opposite view that there was 'no stronger force than the Kaiser'. Other sources see this in either a positive or negative way – but agree on its importance. Source F provides a positive picture of 'an active and vigorous monarchy', while Source I maintains that 'All the important political decisions of the past twelve years have been made by him.' On the negative side, Source H refers to the 'highly dangerous' implications of the Kaiser's personal deterioration, the reasons for which were subsequently suggested by Sigmund Freud (Source K). The one point made by Wehler which is substantiated in the sources is the reference to 'Bonapartism', a theme which is reflected by the Kaiser's reference to putting his 'trust in the army' (Source G).

Substantiating Wehler's argument therefore means going beyond the range of Sources F to K. His view that power resided with the 'traditional oligarchies' is reflected by other historians like Berghahn. The Junker class, or landed aristocracy, combined with the more recently created industrialists to defend their social position against the increasingly threatening proletariat; this process is known as Sammlungspolitik. The Kaiser's regime was therefore dominated by interest groups, operating through a not too efficient administration – or 'polycracy'.

The interpretation of Source L needs to be realigned to allow for at least some influence from the person of the Kaiser. It is unlikely that he would have been entirely manipulable, just as it is possible to exaggerate his personal role. The balance should be somewhere between the individualism stressed in Sources F to K and the determinism of Source L.

5

FOREIGN AND IMPERIAL POLICIES, 1890–1914

BACKGROUND NARRATIVE

The change of personnel after 1890 has been noted in the Background Narrative in Chapter 4. There was also a large-scale change of direction in German foreign policy after 1890, the culmination of which was the outbreak of war in 1914. Indeed, the first stage in this change was partly responsible for Bismarck's resignation. In 1890 Wilhelm II, on the advice of Holstein, refused Russia's request for the renewal of the Reinsurance Treaty, a decision which Bismarck thought amounted to 'criminal negligence and stupidity'. Certainly, the pattern of diplomacy subsequently altered rapidly. Bismarck had aimed to keep Germany as the focal point of European relations. In this his emphasis had always been clear. 'Germany is perhaps the single Great Power in Europe which is not tempted by any objects obtainable only by a successful war. It is in our interest to maintain peace.' After 1890, however, Wilhelm II was emphasising the need for Germany to have 'a place in the sun' – even if this should mean future collisions. The overall approach was therefore to be more assertive and less subtle than it had been under Bismarck.

The most immediate result was the end of Germany's tenuous connection with Russia as the latter now gravitated towards France. By a treaty signed in 1893 and ratified in 1894 they agreed to support each other in the event of an attack by Germany or Austria-

Hungary. Bismarck's network of alliances based *on* Germany now had its counterpart aimed *at* Germany. This greatly reduced the options still available.

There remained, however, one area of flexibility. During the 1890s Britain remained outside the alliance system, in a state described – with dubious accuracy – as 'splendid isolation'. Previously Britain had been peripheral to Germany's diplomacy in Europe. After 1890, however, the relationship between Britain and Germany became crucial. This had both negative and positive aspects, and the Kaiser expressed both admiration for and resentment of Britain. During the 1890s Germany accelerated her colonial policy and greatly increased the pressure on Britain's worldwide interests. This approach soon came to be known as Weltpolitik. In 1894 she refused to compromise with Britain over the Samoan Islands and challenged Britain's Congolese Treaty. In 1896 the Kaiser sent a provocative telegram to President Kruger congratulating the Boers on having dealt with the threat of the Jameson Raid, itself a serious embarrassment to the British government. Between 1899 and 1902, Germany provided moral support to the Boers in their struggle against Britain.

Meanwhile, Germany was also extending her interests in the Balkans and the Middle East, with the ultimate aim of completing a rail link between Berlin and Baghdad. Towards the end of the 1890s Tirpitz also recommended the establishment of a large German navy: this would force Britain to protect home waters at the expense of her extensive imperial commitments. The naval race intensified after the turn of the century and, by 1914, Germany had constructed thirteen Dreadnoughts to Britain's nineteen. Despite – perhaps because of – this competition, there were several agreements attempted between Germany and Britain. One was the Anglo-German Agreement on Portugal's colonies (1898), another the Anglo-German China Agreement of 1900. There were also negotiations in 1898, 1899 and 1901 for a more substantive alliance between Germany and Britain. But these came to nothing, since neither power was prepared to offer what the other wanted.

Instead, the diplomatic situation steadily deteriorated for Germany after 1901. In 1902 Britain found an ally in Japan and, in 1904, proceeded to patch up her colonial differences with France in the Anglo-French Entente (1904), which guaranteed France a free hand in Morocco and Britain in Egypt. Any chance of exploiting their mutual antagonism to Germany's benefit had now gone. In fact, the colonial dimension now worked *against* Germany and actually drove Britain closer to the side of France. This was largely the result of Germany's intrusion into Morocco on two occasions. The first, in 1905–06, led to open British support for France against Germany at the Algeçiras Conference. The second, sparked in 1911 when Germany sent a warship to Agadir, led to the tightening of the Entente into something resembling an alliance.

Meanwhile, the Kaiser had been trying to break up the Franco-Russian alliance by detaching the latter. In 1905 he and Nicholas II signed the Björkö Agreement to the effect that Russia and Germany would assist each other if either was attacked by a third power. This, however, made a nonsense of all existing arrangements and the ministers of both rulers made sure that it was never ratified. Instead, Germany found that Russia was to sort out imperial differences with Britain by the Anglo-Russian Convention (1907). Gradually, therefore, Germany experienced the tightening bands of counter-alliances and alignments. Increasingly she sought security in military preparations and in complex refinements of the Schlieffen Plan for the invasion of France.

After the Björkö fiasco Germany drew closer to Austria-Hungary, supporting the latter's interest in the Balkans to an extent which would have horrified Bismarck – since the result was bound to be the provocation of Russia. Germany backed Austria's occupation of Bosnia-Herzegovina in 1908 and then gave her a 'blank cheque' to sort out the ethnic difficulties involving the Bosnian Serbs and their relationship with neighbouring Serbia. A crisis developed when, on 28 June 1914, the heir to the Austrian throne, the Archduke Franz Ferdinand, was assassinated in Sarajevo. Germany supported the sending of an ultimatum to Serbia on 23 July, acceptance of which would virtually have amounted to the loss of Serbia's independence. When the latter rejected one of the terms of the ultimatum, Austria-Hungary declared war on Serbia on 28 July. Russia mobilised in support of Serbia on 30 July, whereupon Germany sent an ultimatum to Russia on 31 July and declared war on 1 August. On 3 August Germany declared war on France. Because of the direction of attack dictated by the Schlieffen Plan, German forces entered Belgium, which, in turn, was followed on 4 August by the British declaration of war on Germany. On 6 August Austria-Hungary declared war on Russia while Italy, although connected to Germany and Austria-Hungary, remained neutral in 1914.

This background raises two major issues. What were the influences behind the course taken by German foreign policy between 1890 and 1914? And to what extent was Germany responsible for the outbreak of war in 1914?

ANALYSIS (1): WHAT WERE THE MAIN INFLUENCES BEHIND GERMAN FOREIGN POLICY BETWEEN 1890 AND 1914?

There has been a considerable outpouring of interpretations of the influences behind Wilhelmine foreign policy, with the overall slant changing considerably in half a century's research. During the 1950s there was much support for Ritter's view that Germany stumbled towards 1914. This was followed, in the 1960s, by Fischer's argument that Wilhelmine policy was deliberately expansionist and led directly to the outbreak of the First World War. The 1970s saw the establishment of a further dimension, in which external aggression was linked, by Wehler and Berghahn, to domestic policies and pressures. Each stage has elicited its own opposition but, as a result of the debate, it does seem that clearer perspectives are now possible, even if these are more complex than they were in the mid-twentieth century.

The focus of this analysis will be twofold. First, was Wilhelmine policy merely the result of neglecting a still operative Bismarckian system established by Bismarck – or a deliberate attempt to disentangle itself from its impending collapse? And second, was it created by individuals operating conventional political and diplomatic levers – or by the growing pressure of domestic issues?

The development of German foreign policy after 1890 has often been seen as a failure to maintain a system established by Bismarck which was, by 1890, still operable. There is much to commend this. Bismarck had, after all, succeeded in keeping Germany as the focus of the European diplomatic system. He had preserved a state of peace since 1871, which he had seen as being in Germany's best interests. He had taken effective measures to isolate France and prevent an open rift between Austria and Russia. He had made Berlin the conference centre to deal with a European crisis in 1878 and a colonial one in 1884. Finally, he had integrated Germany into a defensive alliance which enabled her to remain 'à trois' on a continent of five powers.

Bismarck's successors destroyed this, partly through negligence, partly through a failure to appreciate the subtle requirements of diplomacy. Negligence was seen immediately in the failure to renew the Reinsurance Treaty with Russia. It was also apparent in the way in which Germany stood back and allowed France to pour investment into Russia's industrial infrastructure between 1891 and 1893; this was followed almost immediately by a military convention in 1893 and the ratification in 1894 of a full alliance between France and Russia, thus realising Bismarck's worst fears that Germany might some day be outflanked. Incompetence was followed by belligerence as the true art of Bismarckian diplomacy was lost. Indeed, during the Wilhelmine period, diplomacy was to become increasingly militarised. It was less about restraint and more about assertiveness; less about manoeuvring and more about forcing; less about flexibility and more about solidity. The result was twofold.

First, Germany drove Britain from the periphery of European diplomacy into its centre. The pursuit of Weltpolitik from 1897 onwards alienated Britain at the very time when Anglo-German accord should have been a real possibility. While Germany confined most of her interest to Europe, Britain's natural rivals were France, who pressed British interests in Africa, and Russia, who threatened the British presence in the Indian subcontinent. Germany's pursuit of colonial aims could not but become the main threat to British interests. The late 1890s saw no subtle and flexible colonialism through France as a surrogate. Instead, it was a blatant threat, the more serious because it was allied to the rapid expansion of the German navy established by the 1898 Navy Law. The effect was to force Britain back to Europe and to seek accommodation on colonial issues, first with France in the Anglo-French Entente (1904), then with Russia by the Convention of 1907.

Second, German action helped to tighten the Ententes into a *de facto* alliance. When Germany attempted to undermine the French position in Morocco in 1905, Britain provided close diplomatic support for French interests at the Algeçiras Conference (1906). Similarly, sending a warship to Agadir in 1911 provoked Britain and France into making military and naval arrangements for joint exercises and action in the event of war. Finally, providing Austria-Hungary with a 'blank cheque' in her treatment of the issue of Bosnia-Herzegovina, annexed in 1908, was tantamount to stoking up tensions in the Balkans rather than releasing them. In short, the Kaiser's regime did everything that Bismarck had sought to prevent. It had allowed France and Russia to come together; it had driven Britain back into Europe by threatening her on the periphery; and it had established a link between the confrontations of the powers and the dangers of the Balkans.

This is a serious set of criticisms. Can they be refuted? It would be difficult to do so entirely but there are certain exaggerations in the argument. In the first place, it is possible that foreign policy after 1890 was a reorientation of something that was already failing. Bismarck had merely been trying to fend off an inevitable link between France and Russia. The Reinsurance Treaty had been an act of desperation rather than of considered and calculated coolness. It could easily have lost Germany the support of Austria and blown a hole in the Triple Alliance – without necessarily reconciling Russia permanently. The new regime therefore took the opportunity to disassociate itself from the measure of a now discredited Chancellor before the Austrian government came to hear of its precise terms. As for the neglect which allowed the drift of Russia towards France, this had already started under Bismarck. Before 1887 Germany had been a key investor in Russia, holding some 2.5 billion marks of Russian securities. In 1887, however, there was a ban on the Berlin stock exchange on trading in Russian securities. France merely stepped in where Germany had pulled out. The process was well under way before 1890 and it would have been difficult to reverse. The emergence of a counter-alliance can therefore be seen as something which Bismarck could only delay; he had little chance of preventing it in the longer term. His successor, Caprivi (1890–94), does not therefore deserve the blame for giving up on the inevitable. Nor is it hard to understand the increasing feeling of insecurity which Germany felt as a result of being outflanked in Europe.

What is more difficult to explain is Germany's subsequent policy towards Britain. From most perspectives it appears arbitrary, misjudged and even foolish. Yet there was a certain method to it. It is arguable that foreign policy after 1894 was based on calculation and method – even if these failed to achieve their objectives. The administration was aware of the importance of diplomacy. But since the degree of flexibility had been greatly reduced, what was now needed was a show of strength. For what purpose? Not so much to intimidate Austria and Russia, who had already committed themselves, but to put pressure on Britain, who had not. In the words of a memorandum produced by Tirpitz in 1897, 'England is the opponent against whom we need most urgently to have a certain measure of naval power as a factor of political power.' (1) The intention was to prove to Britain that her security depended more and more on a close relationship with Germany. As an alternative to being forced away from the periphery back to Europe Britain would recognise the need for an alliance with

Germany to safeguard her position in Europe whilst remaining on the periphery. This approach was nearly successful, as negotiations were conducted between the British and German governments between 1899 and 1902. But the gamble eventually failed: according to Herwig (2), while Bismarck had played chess, Wilhelm II played poker. A series of further hands went the same way. Over Morocco in 1905 and 1911, Germany tried to prove to Britain the vulnerable nature of the Anglo-French Entente, only to find that the Entente was tightening into an alliance. In 1905 the Kaiser tried to revive a strategy which was essentially Bismarckian. The Björkö Agreement was very similar to the Reinsurance Treaty in that it sought to detach Russia from both France and Britain and to ensure Russian neutrality in a war not actually provoked by Germany. But the same trick could not be played twice. Germany did not succeed in escaping from her encirclement and, as a result, began to look to military measures. Diplomacy in the periods approaching 1914 and 1890 had in common that they were both failing. The difference is that the Kaiser gave up on it; Bismarck did not.

So far we have discussed whether German diplomacy was, by comparison with the period 1871–90, negative and negligent or more positive, if unsuccessful. Into these two containers can now be poured two further issues. The action – whether negative or positive – was the result of underlying pressures within Germany, as well as being directed by the deliberate policies of the individuals in charge.

According to some historians, there were strong domestic pressures behind the changing direction of German foreign policy after 1890. Instead of seeing Weltpolitik solely in terms of the pursuit of military and naval dominance, it would also be appropriate to think of it as the externalising of domestic pressures. This is certainly the emphasis of the 'structuralists', so labelled because of their emphasis on the influence of the social and economic structure on the development of Weltpolitik. The obvious influence was economic. During the 1890s the economies of Europe's industrial states expanded quickly, which meant a rapid increase in commercial rivalry and a constant search for new markets. In Germany's case this also meant the growing link between the industrial complex and the use abroad of its main product, the navy. The latter, in any case, was very popular, except with the political left and with the narrowly based and elitist command within the land army. The reason for this was that the development of a navy was seen as a means of completing unification. Because it was an expression of *German* power, it effectively Germanised Prussia, whereas the earlier achievements of the army had really seen the Prussianising of Germany. Not surprisingly, the navy had strong support from those elements, like the Centre Party, which wanted to dilute the influence of Prussia within Germany. This explains why they voted in favour of the Navy Laws in the Reichstag. The expansion of the navy and the growth of Weltpolitik were also immensely popular with the middle classes and with that part of the proletariat which, as in Britain, came to identify with the patriotism that enhanced power and importance engendered. Among fringe groups, this developed along more dubious lines. Layton argues that 'The idealistic nationalism of unification was giving way to the ideas of Social Darwinism and the unending struggle between nations.' (3) This reflects the views of several German historians that pressure groups such as the Pan-German League were motivated by racism and anti-Semitism. At first their emphasis was on overseas expansion but there was also a strong incipient feel for eastward expansion, a point developed especially by Fischer. This eventually linked up with the Lebensraum idea of Hitler, arguably the logical long-term aim of Nazism.

The pressures emphasised by the 'structuralists' should not, however, be allowed to obscure the very real influence of individuals on the formation and implementation of foreign policy. Of greatest importance was the Kaiser himself. According to Lerman, 'He played a central role in determining the policies which eventually led to the Empire's collapse.' (4) He was also more ambitious and impetuous than his predecessors. He modelled himself on Frederick the Great (1740–86) and subordinated the political to the military, giving preference to the army and navy commanders rather than to civilian ministers or the Reichstag. After all, he believed, 'the soldiers and the army, and not the decisions of parliaments, forged the German Reich'. (5) Overall, Wilhelm might be considered important for two reasons. He was the main agent for channelling the ideas, generally produced by others, for the pursuit of Weltpolitik. And, at the same time, he ensured a strong military hold on the political establishment. This is important because it allowed an easy transition from diplomacy to war – defined a century earlier by the Prussian theorist Clausewitz as 'the continuation of policy by other means'.

Wilhelm II presided over foreign policy in a way which had not been attempted by his two predecessors. He exerted considerable influence over his four Chancellors: Caprivi (1890–94), Hohenlohe (1894–1900), Bülow (1900–09) and Bethmann Hollweg (1909–17). At the same time, he was highly receptive to the views of a core of advisers. On the recommendation of Holstein, he abandoned the Reinsurance Treaty in 1890 and, in 1897, took a definite decision to pursue the policy of Tirpitz for Weltpolitik reinforced by naval building. He was especially won over by the argument of Tirpitz that Germany's naval programme would force Britain to 'concede to Your Majesty such a measure of maritime influence which will make it possible for Your Majesty to conduct a great overseas policy'. (6) Weltpolitik did not, therefore, appear spontaneously; it was created.

The increasingly belligerent tone of German policies after 1900 also owed much to the Kaiser's commitment to the interests of the army. He left a powerful military stamp on the government, which was bound to impress itself also on foreign policy. He always appeared in military uniform and surrounded himself with military rather than civilian officials. It is not therefore surprising that he eventually moved away from the diplomatic conception of Europe to the military one. It has been shown, for example, that the German Foreign Ministry had an unofficial parallel set of officials who were connected with the army and who conducted much of the key diplomatic business. All this gives the impression of at least some deliberation.

Less planned, but equally important, were Wilhelm II's occasional flights of fancy. The best example of this was the interview he gave to the *Daily Telegraph* in 1908. In this he argued that public opinion in Germany was strongly anti-British and that he alone stood between it and confrontation with Britain. In fact, this particular incident was counterproductive for the Kaiser's power, since he was subsequently persuaded by the Reichstag and Bülow to adopt a more restrained and constitutional approach to public pronouncements. Nevertheless, his power remained, if not absolute, at least central, and he continued to lend his ear to the military. This was to be of vital importance in the development of the crisis after the Sarajevo assassination.

Some historians see a conflict between the 'structuralist' and 'individual' explanations behind Wilhelm's foreign policy. This does not have to be the case, since there are several clear examples of the two overlapping. There seems to have been at least an element of deliberation in the projection of domestic tensions. There was certainly an awareness within the administration of a growing social stalemate and a build up of internal pressure by 1896. Caprivi's New Course in domestic policy had been meant to reconcile and unite various sectors, such as the Social Democrats and the Centre Party, with the regime. By 1894 this had run into trouble and Caprivi's resignation had been followed by a conservative backlash which could well have precipitated a crisis. The underlying problem was that Germany's industrial growth had created a massive working class which had still not been won over to the regime. The failure of the New Course was therefore followed by a deliberate attempt to externalise pressures by converting class confrontation and party feuding into patriotism through pride in Empire. Bülow, then Foreign Minister, said in 1897: 'I am putting the main emphasis on foreign policy. Only a successful foreign policy can help to reconcile, pacify, rally, unite.' (7) This would have several advantages. It would encourage the aristocracy and the Conservative Party to seek political fulfilment in imperialism and forget their hopes for an onslaught on the Reichstag. In turn, the middle classes would become less obsessive about parliamentary issues and would respond instead to the economic opportunities offered by imperial expansion. Above all, the government hoped to win more widespread popular support for the monarchy by mobilising the masses. Hence, according to Bülow, 'We must unswervingly wrestle for the souls of our workers' through a policy which 'mobilises the best patriotic forces' and 'appeals to the highest national emotions'. (8)

Hence, as Wehler maintains, 'The true significance of Wilhelmine "world policy" can, it seems, be appreciated only if viewed from the perspective of social imperialism. Its precipitate character should not obscure the fact that it was based on the deliberate and calculated use of foreign policy as an instrument for achieving domestic political ends.' (9) Wehler emphasises the 'conscious intentions' of the 'decision makers'. These interacted with and channelled the forces operating below the surface. Individuals could therefore use the structures but could not create them – any more than the structures could control the individuals.

Questions

1. Did those in charge of foreign policy after 1890 destroy a thriving Bismarckian system?
2. Was German foreign policy after 1890 fundamentally influenced by domestic pressures?

ANALYSIS (2): TO WHAT EXTENT WAS GERMANY RESPONSIBLE FOR THE OUTBREAK OF THE FIRST WORLD WAR?

There is a general consensus among historians that Germany carried the main share of the responsibility for the outbreak of the First World War. This does not remove all question of involvement by other powers: Russia and France showed a remarkable willingness to be provoked. Russia was riding on a wave of pan-Slavism, which was bound to clash with German and Austrian interests in the Balkans, as well as having in place a major rearmament programme which was due for completion in 1917. France, according to Poincaré in 1912, 'does not want a war: but she does not fear it'. Both countries had complex war plans to allow for mobilisation at short notice and it was, of course, Russia who mobilised first. Austria, too, must take a share of the responsibility for the start of the conflict through her harsh ultimatum to Serbia which provoked the Russian response.

Yet the acknowledgement that Germany's responsibility was not unique does not necessarily negate the possibility that it was predominant. The focal point of the argument is the response of Germany to the crises which occurred during the three years before 1914, over Morocco (1911), the Balkan Wars (1912–13) and the immediate aftermath of the Sarajevo assassination (July 1914). There are two main approaches for pursuing this. One is that Germany exploited these crises in a deliberate search for war as the means of fulfilling expansionist aims. The other is that Germany had reached a position by 1914 where she was trapped diplomatically and tried to find a way out – even if that involved recourse to war.

There has always been a school of thought that the First World War was provoked by Germany in pursuit of hegemonist aims. This was initially a political statement, contained within the Treaty of Versailles (1919), Article 231 of which affirmed the responsibility 'of Germany and her allies' for the hostilities. The Allied Commission on War Guilt maintained, after a search by historians of the various chancelleries of Europe, that 'The War was premeditated by the Central Powers' and that it was 'the result of acts deliberately committed in order to make it unavoidable'. (10) This is, however, a version of history which has been politicised to justify a diplomatic treaty and polemicised to make the justification sound irrefutable. It was to be expected, therefore, that from the 1920s onwards German historians should have launched a counter-campaign to relieve Germany of the sole responsibility for the outbreak of the war. Hence, France, Russia and even Britain were assigned their own individual roles in the origins of the conflict. The debate then moved along the lines of collective criteria rather than individual responsibility, with the focus on secret alliance systems, the build up of weapons and the production of ever more complex railway timetables to implement inflexible war plans. Preparing against war, in other words, helped provoke it: a collective accident occurred because of the absence of effective controls.

The case for aggression was reactivated in the 1960s by Fischer and it has been German historians who have since been the focus of this new wave of interpretation, now shorn of any political considerations and able to focus entirely on historical reassessment. From 1912 onwards, it is argued, Germany actively worked for war, especially from the time of the 1912 'War Council'. During the period immediately following the assassination at Sarajevo, Germany put pressure on Austria to deal with Serbia, knowing full well that this would result in the outbreak of war. But this was *not* the start of the process. Behind Germany's reaction to these crises was a longer-term momentum towards expansion, the true extent of which was shown by the war plans developed by Germany during the First World War. These included economic dominance over Belgium, Holland and France; hegemony over the western parts of Russia such as Courland, Livonia, Estonia, Lithuania and Poland; control over the Balkans, including Bulgaria, Romania and Turkey; the absorption of Austria and the creation of a Greater Germany; and expansion over the entire Mediterranean.

Driving this momentum were powerful internal influences. The most important of these was the failure of the ruling German elites – the traditional agrarians and the new industrialists – to adjust to the major political, social and economic changes taking place within Germany. As we have seen in Analysis 1, internal tensions were externalised in the form of Weltpolitik. Part of the process was a new focus on Europe, as pan-Germanic groups were encouraged to press for expansion in eastern Europe. War in Europe was therefore the logical next stage to Weltpolitik and would provide the means of resolving Germany's internal tensions while bringing about conquest abroad. Indeed, these very tensions provided the impetus necessary for conquest. Thus, in Fischer's view, the crises of 1911–13 and July 1914 were merely opportunities for Germany to press ahead with a preconceived aim based on a longer-term momentum for expansion: the war was provoked by Germany. Indeed, the crisis of July 1914 was deliberately turned into a war in pursuit of Germany's quest for world domination.

There are, however, several problems with such an approach. First, the aims which developed during the war may not necessarily have been those which started it. They could well have grown during the second half of 1914 and in 1915. The Fischer thesis is part of a broader view which connects with Nazi Germany. In a sense it is too closely structured. There may well be elements of continuity but the whole argument comes close in places to being deterministic. Similarly, the connection between domestic policy and assertiveness abroad is one thing. But to extend this into the search for war is quite another. War had an uncomfortable habit of generating revolution in defeat, while even victory could bring social change which the elites could not be certain of being able to control. Whatever happened, the equilibrium would be upset. War could therefore act as a means of bouncing the externalised domestic problems back into the domestic sphere – with redoubled force. Would the elites have wanted to risk this?

It makes more sense, therefore, to look for an alternative explanation. This could still combine the ingredients of aggressive diplomacy and the ready resort to the military solution – but without the same emphasis on deliberate provocation. This is the approach favoured by most German historians, including Wehler, Mommsen and Berghahn, who prefer the notion of the calculated risk to that of planned aggression. It is possible to develop an argument in support of this which involves several integrated stages.

German aggression was born of fear of encirclement. This helped shape Germany's whole approach to international diplomacy. The encirclement took two forms. One was the Franco-Russian Alliance of 1894, subsequently enlarged by the Anglo-French Entente of 1904 and the Anglo-Russian Convention and Triple Entente (1907). The other comprised the diplomatic reverses suffered by Germany between 1911 and 1913. This fear of encirclement was exacerbated by concern that the Entente powers would soon catch up with and overtake Germany's military strength. Reservations about Russia were especially strong. Bethmann Hollweg said in 1914 that 'It grows and grows and hangs over us ever more heavily like a nightmare.' (11) According to Jagow: 'In a few years, according to expert opinion, Russia will be ready to strike. Then she will crush us with the weight of her soldiers.' (12) Concern about France was equally strong. The French rearmament plan was well under way and was narrowing the gap with Germany.

Meanwhile, encirclement was being tightened by the threat of diplomatic humiliation. For one thing Germany herself had experienced a serious reverse over the Agadir Crisis of 1911. This had resulted in loss of face and a tightening of the Anglo-French Entente (1904) into a de facto military alliance through the Anglo-French naval manoeuvres and agreements. For another, Germany's ally had also been put on the spot as a result of the Balkan Wars. The outcome of these was an enlarged Serbia, which was clearly becoming a Russian surrogate and which would pose an increased threat to Austria's control over the Bosnian Serb population of Bosnia-Herzegovina, annexed as recently as 1908. This would sooner or later create additional crises to put further pressure on Germany.

How should Germany respond to this situation? There were actually historical precedents which were very much within the Prussian tradition that was so dear to Wilhelm II. These were a combination of diplomacy and war, a relatively easy transition from one to the other – and then back again. Frederick the Great (1740–86) had used precisely this method during the War of the Austrian Succession (1740–48), the Diplomatic Revolution (1755–56) and the Seven Years' War (1756–63). In the process, he had managed to fend off France, Austria and Russia and to lead Prussia to territorial enhancement. At the end of the eighteenth century the Prussian military strategist von Clausewitz had formally articulated what Frederick had long been practising – that 'war is the continuation of policy by other means'. Bismarck had revived the Prussian tradition during the 1860s, and moved easily between war and diplomacy during the unification of Germany. Why should Wilhelm II, an ardent admirer of Frederick the Great and of the earlier Bismarck, be any different in his approach? The Prussian military tradition was based on rapid victory hard on the heels of diplomatic breakdown which would, in turn, lead to a diplomatic breakthrough. The situation had developed by 1914 which seemed to require yet another re-enactment of a traditional response.

The military groundwork had certainly been carefully prepared. The Schlieffen Plan assumed the encirclement of Germany and devised a means of breaking it. Faced with the simultaneous mobilisation of Russia and France, Germany would attack France first and then engage Russia. The first would be defeated rapidly because it would be attacked through Belgium, while Russia could be dealt with later because it would take longer to mobilise. The original version became progressively refined until it had locked into place the entire German railway network to deliver German troops to the front with maximum speed and efficiency. Diplomacy could therefore be continued, at a moment's notice, by other means.

Or, alternatively, the breakdown of diplomacy could be redeemed by a successful war. This was the situation in which Germany found herself between 1912 and 1914. There was no long-term pressure for war, but rather a flexible approach to the possibilities of war or peace. The 1912 'War Council' meeting showed a division of opinion as to whether Germany should go to war: some of the military favoured war, 'the sooner the better', while others preferred to hold off. Ultimately the decision was taken by the Chancellor, Bethmann Hollweg. He has often been projected as the hapless victim of an aggressive military establishment, pushed into a course of action in July 1914 which was bound to lead to war. It actually makes more sense to see him as locked into the traditional military–diplomatic interplay. Hence, his answer was to pursue a 'diagonal policy' between war and peace. In doing this he sought diplomatic victory for Germany and Austria over the Serbian Crisis – but at the high risk of war. Bethmann Hollweg wrote on 29 July 1914 to the German Ambassador in Vienna: 'It is solely a matter of finding a means of making the realization of Austria-Hungary's aims possible . . . without at the same time unleashing a world war, and if this is in the end not to be avoided, to bring about the best possible conditions under which we may wage it.' (13)

A comparison may perhaps be made with the outbreak of the Second World War. In both cases there appears to have been a growing momentum, indicated by the 'War Council' meeting of 1912 and the meeting summoned by Hitler in 1937 (recorded in the Hossbach Memorandum). In both cases there was an emphasis on the growing danger of the Allies, especially since these were extending the scope of their rearmament.

Yet this comparison also shows the difference in the build up to the two conflicts. Before the outbreak of war in September 1939 Hitler had already extended Germany's frontiers by annexing Austria, the Sudetenland and Bohemia. Wilhelm II had annexed nothing. Hitler invaded Poland in September 1939 as the next phase of an expansionist drive. Wilhelm II invaded Belgium in August 1914 as a means of implementing the Schlieffen Plan which would enable Germany to respond effectively to a war on two fronts. In both cases Germany was aggressive. But there is a clear difference in the type of aggression. Hitler was intensifying the momentum which he had already created, whereas Wilhelm II was starting up the momentum. Hitler was moving from one military phase to the next; Wilhelm was switching to the military phase from diplomacy. Hitler was driving forwards; Wilhelm was *escaping* forwards. In this sense Germany was largely responsible for both wars, but the basic intention differed between them. Fischer's hypothesis therefore applies the momentum of the Third Reich to the Second, which is bound to result in a direct evolution between the Second and the Third. Not all historians are convinced by these links.

Questions

1. Consider the arguments for and against Germany deliberately provoking the First World War for 'hegemonist' reasons.
2. Consider the arguments for and against Germany bringing on the First World War by 'escaping forwards'.

SOURCES

1. THE ABANDONMENT OF BISMARCK'S FOREIGN POLICY

Source A: the view of General von Waldersee, 19 December 1891.

We make great sacrifices to bind Italy and Austria to us, whereas previously we were in a position to let them beg us to protect them. Herein lies the great difference between the policies of Bismarck and of Caprivi.

Source B: from a newspaper comment on the ministry of Caprivi, 1894.

General von Caprivi has exhibited the foremost quality of statesmanship in knowing both when to follow and when to relinquish the policy of the past. From Prince Bismarck's hands he took up the strings of the frame of the Triple Alliance, and, working on broader lines, has made it more tenacious than ever. He has given it a capacity, practically boundless, for absorbing every healthy element in Europe tending to the confirmation of peace.

Source C: Military Convention between France and Russia. This was drafted in 1892, approved in 1893 and ratified in 1894.

1   If France is attacked by Germany, or by Italy supported by Germany, Russia shall employ all her available forces to fight Germany.
    If Russia is attacked by Germany, or by Austria supported by Germany, France shall employ all her available forces to fight Germany.
2   In case the forces of the Triple Alliance, or of one of the powers composing it, should mobilize, France and Russia, at the first news of the event and without the necessity of any previous concert, shall mobilize immediately and simultaneously the whole of their forces and shall move them as close as possible to their frontiers.
3   The available forces to be employed against Germany shall be, on the part of France, 1,300,000 men, on the part of Russia, 700,000 or 800,000 men.
    These forces shall engage to the full, with all speed, in order that Germany may have to fight at the same time on the East and on the West.

Source D: advice given to Kaiser Wilhelm II in 1899 by Admiral Tirpitz.

Apart from the, for us, by no means prospectless conditions of battle, England, for general political reasons and from the purely sober perspective of the businessman, will have lost every inclination to attack us and as a result will concede such a measure of maritime prestige to Your Majesty and will enable Your Majesty to practise a grand overseas policy.

Source E: An article in the periodical _Der Tag_, 15 December 1912, by Professor Martin Spahn, a pan-German.

The German Reich under his [Wilhelm II's] leadership has broken out of the confines of Prussian foreign policy. That is the Kaiser's contribution and one which lifts him high above all his German contemporaries in significance for the nation. But the nation has still not placed itself sufficiently strongly behind the Kaiser . . . And this situation will not really change until it is made clear to the nation again that in terms of foreign policy the entire region from the North Sea to the Adriatic must be regarded now as ever as a single entity to be covered by us jointly with Austria.

Questions

1. (i) Explain the reference to the 'Triple Alliance' (Source B). (2 marks)
   (ii) Explain the meaning of 'broken out of the confines of Prussian foreign policy' (Source E). (2 marks)
2. What is the main difference between Sources A and B in their interpretation of the foreign policies of Bismarck and Caprivi? How would you explain this difference? (4 marks)
*3. What can be inferred from Source C about the change in the way in which France and Russia viewed Germany after 1890? (5 marks)
4. Compare the language and tone of Sources B and E. (4 marks)
5. 'The adjustment of Bismarck's foreign policy after 1890 was dangerous and disastrous.' Taking account of Sources A to E, and your own knowledge, do you agree with this view? (8 marks)

Worked answer

*3. _[Making inferences from a source involves working backwards from its text to the situation which made the source necessary. This means that a degree of background knowledge is necessary, but this should emerge through the source.]_

Several changes can be inferred. Clause 1 shows that Germany was now considered the main threat by Russia, which was a change, as well as by France, which was not. Previously Russian policy had, through the Reinsurance Treaty of 1887, been to neutralise Germany in the event of a war between Austria and Russia; in the Franco-Russian Alliance it was assumed that Austria would merely play a supporting role to an aggressive Germany. As far as France was concerned, the main change was that Germany was perceived sufficiently menacing to involve a commitment to support Russia, even though this meant an undertaking, by Clause 3, to contribute more troops than Russia. Finally, both Russia and France were, for the first time, consciously using the geographical vulnerability of Germany to their favour: this is shown in the promise of immediate mobilisation (Clause 2) to 'engage to the full, with all speed' (Clause 3). Overall, France and Russia now considered Germany sufficiently threatening for them both to take the initiative.

2. GERMANY AND THE OUTBREAK OF WAR IN 1914

Source F: from a letter from the leader of the National Liberal Party, Basserman, to his party colleague, Schiffer, 1914.

Things are not going well. The anti-German movement in Russia is becoming stronger, the French are getting more and more cocky . . . Bethmann said to me with fatalistic resignation: 'if there is a war with France, the last Englishman will march against us' . . . We are drifting towards the world war.

Source G: from a weekly paper, *Das Grössere Deutschland*, established in the spring of 1914.

Any intelligent person must realise that France cannot bear this burden [three-year conscription] for long and that the adoption of such a measure can only be comprehensible if those involved say: this will be the last great strenuous effort before the decision. The most the French can bear is a few more years of three-year conscription and when this period is over the acceleration of Russian deployment will also be complete. And what will happen then? Does anyone believe that after the great sacrifice she has made France would draw the line by reverting to two-year conscription and Russia would let the grass grow on her new railways? Or should we perhaps let Austria or Turkey be sacrificed for us?

Source H: a report, from the Austrian Ambassador in Berlin to the Foreign Minister of Austria-Hungary, 5 July 1914. This is his summary of a conversation he had had with Kaiser Wilhelm II.

The Kaiser authorised me to inform our gracious majesty that we might in this case, as in all others, rely upon Germany's full support . . . he did not doubt in the least that Herr von Bethmann Hollweg would agree with him. Especially as far as our action against Serbia was concerned. But it was the Kaiser's opinion that this action must not be delayed. Russia's attitude will no doubt be hostile, but for this he had for years prepared, and should a war between Austria-Hungary and Russia be unavoidable, we might be convinced that Germany, our old faithful ally, would stand at our side. Russia at the present time was in no way prepared for war, and would think twice before it appealed to arms . . . if we had really recognised the necessity of warlike action against Serbia, the Kaiser would regret it if we did not make use of the present moment, which is all in our favour.

Source I: from a letter by von Jagow (German Secretary of State) to Prince Lichnowsky (German Ambassador in London), 18 July 1914.

Austria no longer intends to tolerate the sapping activities of the Serbians, and just as little does she intend to tolerate longer the continuously provocative attitude of her small neighbour at Belgrade . . . She fully realizes that she has neglected many opportunities, and that she is still able to act, though in a few years she may no longer be able to do so. Austria is now going to force a showdown with Serbia and has told us so. During the whole Balkan crisis we mediated successfully in the interest of peace, without forcing Austria to passivity at any of the critical moments . . . We neither could nor should attempt to stay her hand. If we should do that, Austria would have the right to reproach us . . . with having deprived her of her last chance of political rehabilitation. And then the process of her wasting away and of her internal decay would be still further accelerated. Her standing in the Balkans would be gone for ever. You will undoubtedly agree with me that the absolute establishment of the Russian hegemony in the Balkans is, indirectly, not permissible, even for us.

Questions

1. (i)   Who was 'Bethmann' (Source F)? (1 mark)
    (ii) Explain the reference to 'the sapping activities of the Serbians' (Source I). (2 marks)
    (iii) By what phrase is the promise of support to Austria (in Source H) commonly known? (1 mark)

2. To what extent do Sources F and G agree on the perceived threats from Russia and France? (4 marks)

*3. To what extent does it appear that Source H had an influence on Source I? (5 marks)

4. What questions might the historian wish to ask about Sources H and I as evidence for Germany's involvement in the outbreak of the First World War? (5 marks)

5. Using the Sources and your own knowledge, do you agree that the German government was forced into war in 1914? (7 marks)

Worked answer

*3. *[The answer to this question needs a close attention to chronology. Source H was produced on 5 July, Source I on 18 July. Since Source H focuses on the view of the Kaiser, Source I can be seen as a basic attempt to fall into line with his view. On the other hand, some discrepancy should be included, given the wording 'to what extent' in the question.]*

The main influence apparently exerted by Source H on Source I is the stiffening of Austria's resolve to deal with Serbia as a result of the guarantee, by the Kaiser, of Germany's support. There is a direct parallel between the arguments of the two documents, showing that the Kaiser's views must have been officially repeated since his conversation with the Austrian Ambassador (Source H) and consolidated among German ministers and diplomats. Both emphasise the need for Austria to deal with the problem of Serbia. Source H emphasises that 'this action must not be delayed' and that it would be regrettable 'if we did not make use of the present moment'. Source I repeats the argument that there could be no further toleration of 'sapping activities of the Serbians'. Furthermore, Austria had been reinforced by the German guarantee 'to force a showdown with Serbia'.

On two issues the parallel between Sources H and I are less obvious. Source H refers to the current weakness of Russia, the main obstacle to Austrian action, while Source I stresses the threat of Russian 'hegemony' if action were *not* taken by Austria. Secondly, the guarantee of German support is more explicit in Source H than in I. On the other hand, the whole assumption behind Source I would have made little sense without that support being taken for granted.

6

ECONOMY AND SOCIETY, 1871–1914

ANALYSIS (1): HOW AND WHY DID THE GERMAN ECONOMY EXPAND BETWEEN 1871 AND 1914?

The German industrial revolution occurred somewhat later than those of Great Britain and Belgium, the first two states to experience a transformation of their economic infrastructure. But when it did happen, German industrialisation was more rapid and intensive. The overall effect was the transformation of a primarily agrarian economy into Europe's leading industrial power, second in the world only to the United States. During the period 1867–1914 overall production increased eight times; by comparison, that of France increased three times and that of Britain doubled. The usual measure for industrial growth is steel production: Germany's increased from 0.2 million metric tons in 1871 to 17.9 million in 1913. The equivalent figures for Britain were 0.3 million and 7.4 million and for France 0.1 million and 4.6 million. The result was the transformation of the balance between agriculture and industry. In the 1880s agriculture accounted for up to 40 per cent of the total GNP, with industry up to 35 per cent, changing by 1913 to 25 per cent and 45 per cent respectively. In the meantime, the commercial and service sectors remained consistent at about 30 per cent.

The process started to be noticeable around 1850, then gathered momentum until the mid-1870s, after which Germany, like most other countries, experienced a depression of varying intensity. This, according to Mommsen, gave way to a period of 'accelerating economic expansion' between 1896 and 1913. (1) This pattern resembles a zig-zag; Berghahn's observation is that although the macroeconomic trend was upward, 'the economy was prone to overheat or to sputter from time to time'. (2)

The rapidity of this overall growth-rate was due to a number of interrelated factors. One was the long-term influence of Prussia on the rest of Germany. The initiative seized by Prussia, as opposed to Austria, in establishing the Zollverein between herself and the smaller German states not only provided the infrastructure for political unification but set in motion the rapid expansion of trade and industry in central Europe. Prussia had also seen considerable changes and progress in agriculture, which had similarly contributed to the process. Industrialisation depends in part on capital accumulation, which had initially taken place during the first half of the nineteenth century in the agrarian sector. Thereafter, the pace of industrialisation outstripped that of agriculture. But this was not due to any agricultural decline. Instead, agriculture continued to act as a stimulus, with heightened demand for threshing machines (of which there were 268,000 by 1882 and 947,000 by 1907) and steam threshers, which increased from 75,500 to 489,000 during the same period. Prussia also had considerable advantages in terms of natural resources. This applied especially to the enormous coal and iron deposits in the Rhineland, given to Prussia by the Treaty of Vienna in 1815, and to the extensive potassium salt deposits near Halle, upon which was built Germany's chemical industry, which included such giants as Bayer at Leverkusen.

Germany also had certain advantages in being among the second wave of industrialising economies. This meant the process was initially derivative, based upon adaptations of and improvements on the experience of the earlier changes made in Britain and Belgium; Germany could therefore benefit from their mistakes. Hence Britain exercised a considerable influence over developments in German mining and textiles, and Belgium over the German chemical industry. Germany then proved capable of becoming increasingly self-sufficient as home-based research took over from imported ideas, thereby accelerating the pace of industrialisation. By the turn of the century, German research was foremost in Europe: 6,449 patents were taken out in 1900, indicating the range of German inventiveness. Some applications for patents were made by individuals, but the majority were the result of organised research and development within the companies. Their growing dependence on trained scientists was, in turn, facilitated by ever-increasing state involvement in scientific and technical education: expenditure on these areas increased tenfold in real terms between 1870 and 1914. Particularly important in the process were

technical high schools. By 1913, each one of these was ⌐
more engineering graduates than all the universities of the
Kingdom together. The result was a steady flow into the research
development departments in industrial firms of highly qualified peopⅼ⌐
who, in the words of Berghahn, could 'turn inventions into new
products'. (3) At the same time, German scientists always kept an
eye on what was happening across the Atlantic, to see what ideas
and processes could be used from the United States. The sheer weight
of this research tends to hide the achievements of individual German
entrepreneurs, whereas in Britain these stood out. There were, however, notable exceptions, especially Siemens, whose invention of the
dynamo gave an enormous boost to the electricity industry from
the 1870s onwards, culminating in the predominance of the combines
of Allgemeine Elektrizitäts-Gesellschaft (AEG) and Siemens-Schukert.

Research and technical inventions flourished in Germany because of
a huge financial and banking infrastructure. In fact, banking and industrialisation were closely interconnected. For example, Deutsche Bank,
Commerz-und-Disconto Bank and Dresdner Bank were linked with
Siemens and AEG. Such connections greatly increased the sense of
security in forward and strategic planning, which was a vital requirement
for future expansion.

Another factor in Germany's rapid growth was the structural
organisation which took place within industry. It became increasingly
apparent during the period of depression that there was great benefit
in co-operation between businesses rather than open rivalry. This took
several forms. First, associations were established which would
involve several businesses for lobbying purposes. These put influence
on the government. They were, for example, particularly responsible
for the government's decision to impose tariffs between 1878 and
1879. This reduced the competition from abroad during a period of
limited world markets. Second, many firms took the logical next
step, which was to reduce internal competition within Germany. This
meant the emergence of agreements which were more characteristic
of German industry than anywhere else: they took the form of cartels.
These increased, initially in response to the depression, from eight
in 1875 to seventy by 1887. They were arrangements backed by
law and any attempts by members to underprice their commodities
would involve legal litigation. The cartels were so successful that,
even though they had been established to ride out the period of
depression, they were renewed once the period of economic growth
resumed after 1895: hence the number had reached 300 by 1900 and
673 by 1910.

Such structures also ensured the development of a disciplined workforce. Each of the newly developed industries based its rules on a semi-military regime. The employers also had the advantage in that the ever increasing demand for workers was satisfied by a rapid increase in population. In total the increase was from 41 million in 1871 to 65.3 million by 1911. The growth in the cities was disproportionately high, a natural increase in birthrate being accompanied by a large-scale migration from the countryside. It was the case that literally millions of people were on the move, in search of jobs within the new industries. In most cases, therefore, firms could afford to be tough in their terms of employment, while the development of the cartel system actively prevented competition between firms in offering higher wages.

Overall, it is hardly surprising that the pace of German industrialisation should have been so rapid or that exports should have increased from 2.9 billion marks in 1880 to 10.1 billion by 1913. In its promotion of research, government financing and cartelisation, German industry rapidly took the lead in Europe, while the control of the labour force meant that there was relatively little disruption from industrial unrest. Such developments were not without their price; this was the growth of social problems and confrontations, a theme which is taken up in Analysis 2.

Questions

1. Why was the industrialisation of Germany during the Second Reich so rapid?
2. Can Germany's industrialisation be described as 'revolutionary'?

ANALYSIS (2): WHAT EFFECT DID ECONOMIC CHANGES HAVE ON GERMAN SOCIETY AND POLITICS BETWEEN 1871 AND 1914?

The process of industrialisation inevitably involves some degree of social change. In the case of Germany between 1871 and 1914 there were three general trends. One was the rapid expansion of the working class and their concentration in cities with an ever increasing population. The second was the hardening of the attitudes of the social elites, who refused to allow for any upward social mobility. The third was an increasingly frustrated middle class, caught between the forceful thrust of the working class and the unyielding resistance of the upper levels of society. Industrialisation therefore combined the different dynamics of expansion from below, resistance from above, and fracturing in the middle.

Pressure was exerted from below in the most basic form: the growth of the population from 41 million in 1871 to 65 million by 1911. A substantial proportion of this increase came within the proletariat. It is difficult to see how this could have been *caused* by industrialisation unless there had been a conscious decision to have larger families; in the absence of any effective forms of birth control this would seem unlikely. It is, of course, possible that industrialisation brought a greater degree of occupational stability, along with a more extensive review of the needs of public health – both of which would indirectly have reduced the incidence of infant mortality. But the real impact of industrialisation was on the *distribution* of population. It has been estimated that by 1907 nearly 40 per cent of all Germans had moved from one area to another, mainly from the countryside to the towns. This accounts for the rapid growth of Berlin, Cologne, Essen and Dortmund. There was also a major change in the pattern of occupations. In 1871 the proportions of population employed in agriculture and industry had been 41 per cent and 31 per cent; by 1907 the figures were 35 per cent and 40 per cent respectively. This movement was due to the attractions of the towns and their promise of higher wages than could be earned on the farms. Another factor was the relative decline in the productivity of the Junker estates, which had a knock-on effect on the wages of their labourers. The growing concentration of the workforce in the industrial areas, especially the Ruhr, provided a spur to trade unionism and grass-roots organisations and pressure groups within the SPD. These became increasingly vocal in their demands for social and political reform.

Resisting these was the main priority of Germany's elites. At this level of society there was therefore serious social stagnation: Pulzer refers to 'the dissonance between the economic dynamism of the Reich and the relative stagnation of its social norms and political institutions'. (4) Part of the reason for this was that the very speed of Germany's industrialisation meant that society was less able to adjust to it than in Britain and Belgium, where the process had taken place over a much longer period of time. In Germany industrialisation did not result in social mobility between classes, but rather a stratification of existing structures. The working class, for example, strengthened its identity and expanded its size, while this served to intensify the suspicion of the social elites.

Who were these? One was the traditional and pre-industrial class, landed elites such as the Prussian Junkers. They felt particularly vulnerable since the proportion of agriculture to industry within the total economy was in steady decline. Some of the Junkers were forced to sell off parts of their estates or their townhouses in Berlin. Even so, they managed to maintain a grip on the levers of power. Another was the newly developed class of industrialists. They might have attempted to supersede the Junkers and to establish themselves as the new ruling class. Yet by and large they preferred to co-operate with the Junkers: hence it made sense for them to share power.

This showed itself in practice in several ways. Politically, it influenced the development of the party system. The National Liberals and Free Conservatives increasingly represented the interests and views of the industrialists, while the Conservatives were primarily the party of the Junkers and the agrarian interest. From the early 1880s onwards these tended to co-operate in the defence of the old and new elites; although there were periods of disagreement and political realignment it was generally in their interest to seek a convergence of issues.

There was also much in common between the authoritarian attitudes of the Junkers and the top-down discipline exerted in industrial management methods used in industrialisation. Berghahn argues that the way in which industries developed in the form of cartels was unique to Germany. In particular, it was in contrast to the more liberal focus of the United States, which aimed to pass on the benefits of competition in the form of lower prices for the consumer. In Germany, however, the purpose of the cartels was that the industries themselves should benefit through not having to compete for the attention of the consumer. 'Ultimately, the consumer had to pay and the benefits of mass production were not passed on.' Hence, 'German industry developed into a well-organized, authoritarian producer capitalism.' (5) The development of cartels was also partly about the discipline of the workforce in a semi-military sense. The influence of the Prussian army was apparent in the expectations of industrial management, and the workforce was subject to an authoritarian industrial structure. There were strong political implications as the National Liberals and the Conservatives co-operated with the measures taken against the SPD by Bismarck and his successors.

Caught between the layers of the workforce and the social elites were the middle classes. Here the pressures were applied from both directions – from the expanding working class below them and from the industrialists and Junkers above them. The lower middle class comprised small shopkeepers, artisans and peasant landowners. Their main preoccupation was to retain their class identity and to resist pressures from below to proletarianise them. The professional middle class consisted mainly of civil servants, lawyers and technical advisers in industry. Their concern was that upward social mobility might be blocked by the new elites.

The political implications of this social diversity are threefold. First, the elites sought to externalise the social pressures within Germany by supporting an increasingly active foreign and colonial policy. This became apparent during the administration of Bismarck, although the latter succeeded in controlling its momentum. It was pursued more vigorously from 1897 and further intensified after 1900. The intention was to rally the lower orders and to channel their attention into nationalism through patriotism rather than socialism through internationalism. The political momentum was therefore to pull the lower orders to the right to counteract the lure of the left – whether the Social Democrats in the case of the working class or the progressive faction of the liberals in the case of the middle classes.

The result of this was to be a social fracturing, which was to be of vital importance for the future. The working class became increasingly divided between those who were inclined to revolution and those who preferred to adapt to the political system and to seek reforms within it. This dilemma was represented within the SPD, which developed revolutionary and reformist wings. During the First World War this contrast was accentuated until, by the end of the war, the left wing broke off to form the Spartacists which, in turn, became the Communists, or KPD. The middle class was similarly fractured, with a substantial section seeking political outlet in the fringe movements of the right.

Overall, Germany's economic growth had several quite different effects on the various parts of society. The working class was considerably expanded in size. The elites did their best to impose constraints on this expansion being expressed in political terms. The middle classes were caught between the two. The overall result was a combination of rapid social change, deliberate immobility and fracturing within the working and middle classes. The political repercussions were considerable. The elites took refuge in diversionary policies, which led to the adoption of Weltpolitik, with all its consequent complications. The working and middle classes splintered between radical groupings, which moved towards the fringes of the political spectrum, and moderates, which remained, although in decreased numbers, near the centre. If, at any time, the Reich should give way to another regime, its legacy would be a series of contradictions.

Questions

1. Who gained and who lost from the industrialisation of Germany's economy?
2. Did the industrialisation of Germany promote or impede social mobility?

SOURCES

1. CHANGES IN THE GERMAN ECONOMY, 1871–1913

Source A: population growth in Germany (in 'ooos).

Year	Population	% rural	% urban
1871	41,059	63.9	36.1
1880	45,234	58.6	41.4
1890	49,428	57.5	42.5
1900	56,367	45.6	54.4
1910	64,926	40.0	60.0

Source B: production of coal and steel in Germany (in million metric tons).

Year	Coal	Steel
1871	29.4	0.2
1890	109.3	2.2
1913	191.5	17.9

Source C: the distribution of Germany's labour force (in 'ooos)

Sector	1875	1885	1895	1905	1913
Agriculture	9,230	9,700	9,788	9,926	10,701
Mining	286	345	432	665	863
Industry	5,153	6,005	7,524	9,572	10,857
Transport	349	461	620	901	1,174

Source D: index of Germany's exports and imports by volume (1913=100).

Year	Exports	Imports
1880	22.4	25.5
1885	25.9	31.8
1890	29.8	44.0
1895	31.7	52.0
1900	44.7	63.2
1905	58.2	75.1
1910	77.4	88.3
1913	100.0	100.0

Source E: numbers of students in higher education in Germany.

Year	Universities	Technical universities
1891	27,398	4,209
1902	35,857	13,151
1912	56,830	11,349

Source F: the average earnings of workers in industry, commerce and transport.

Year	Cost of living index (1895=100)	Average annual income (in marks)
1871	105.8	466
1875	112.7	578
1880	104.0	524
1885	98.6	589
1890	102.2	636
1895	100.0	665
1900	106.4	737
1905	112.4	755
1910	124.2	789
1913	129.8	834

Questions

*1. In what two ways might Source A indicate a major change in the population of Germany between 1871 and 1910? (2 marks)

2. To what extent might Sources B and C be used to explain the changes shown in Source A? (4 marks)

3. What do the figures in Source D show of the relative levels of imports and exports in Germany between 1880 and 1913? Suggest one major shortcoming in this source. (5 marks)

4. To what extent do Sources D, E and F prove that there was a rise in the standard of living in Germany between 1880 and 1913? (6 marks)

5. Using the Sources, and your own knowledge, discuss the view that 'between 1871 and 1914 Germany was transformed into an industrial giant at the expense of its agricultural base'. (8 marks)

Worked answer

*1. Source A shows an overall increase in the population between 1871 and 1910, together with a shift from a predominantly rural to a largely urban base.

2. WEALTH, POVERTY AND EMPLOYMENT

Source G: a description by Benjamin Disraeli of the home of Gerson Bleichröder, banker to Bismarck, in the late 1870s.

The banqueting hall, very vast and very lofty, and indeed the whole mansion, is built of every species of rare marble, and where it is not marble it is gold. There was a gallery for the musicians who played Wagner . . . After dinner, we were promenaded through the splendid saloons – and picture galleries, and a ballroom fit for a fairy-tale, and sitting alone on a sofa was a very mean-looking little woman, covered with pearls and diamonds, who was Madame Bleichröder and whom he had married very early in life when he was penniless. She was unlike her husband, and by no means equal to her wondrous fortune.

Figure 1   A photograph of a cellar dwelling in a Berlin
slum, 1905.

Figure 2 A cartoon from a Social Democratic magazine, *Der wahre Jacob* (1891) showing an exhausted Atlas being relieved of his burden. The caption reads 'The workers inherit the earth!'

Source J: from a report by a British Royal Commission on labour conditions in Central Europe, 1893.

The general consensus of opinion in the country as a whole indicates a very great change for the better in the economic condition of the labourer during the past ten or twenty years. He is better fed and better clothed, better educated and better able to procure the means of recreation; nevertheless the migration statistics . . . indicate a continuous movement of the population from the agricultural east to the industrial west. Except in a few southern districts, such as Bavaria, where peculiar conditions prevail, the agrarian question proper, interpreted in Germany to mean the difficulty of procuring a sufficient supply of labour, scarcely exists in the west. With regard to the east, on the contrary... unless some means can be adopted for checking the outflow of the German population, there is every reason to believe that their places will be supplied by an inroad of Slavs... The gulf which separates the employer from the employed in the east, and the lack of opportunity for acquiring land are... mainly responsible for its depopulation.

Source K: from a speech by Caprivi to the Reichstag, 1891. Caprivi was defending his trade treaties.

The working class is bound together with industry most intimately, and we would have neglected our duty if we had not, in concluding these treaties, kept the possibility of preserving our working class, preserving their ability to be productive, steadily before us. Two factors then came up for discussion: first, to procure cheaper foodstuffs. Insofar as that could take place without endangering state interests... the governments [involved in the treaties] have effected the lowering of the tariff which they consider permissible. For the preservation of the working class, however, I regard it as far more essential that work should be found for them. If this were not the more essential question, then the rush of our rural labourers to the cities could hardly be explained... Remunerative jobs will be found if these treaties are accepted. We will find them by means of export. We must export; either we export goods, or we export people. With this mounting population, and without a comparably growing industry, we are not in a position to survive any longer.

Questions

1. (i) Who was Caprivi (Source K)? (1 mark)
   (ii) Name two countries with which Caprivi established a trade treaty. (2 marks)
2. What, for the historian, are the main advantages and disadvantages of Sources G and H as descriptions of living conditions in the Reich? (6 marks)
*3. How much light do Sources H and J throw on Source I? (4 marks)
4. How far is Source K an acknowledgement of the accuracy of Source J's assessment of the problems of the German labour force? (4 marks)
5. To what extent do Sources G to K, and your own knowledge, show that, during the Second Reich, the German people benefited from Germany's economic changes? (8 marks)

Worked answer

*3. By its nature as a political cartoon, Source I is polemical and one-sided. The emphasis is very much on the readiness and willingness of the working class to take over. Sources H and J can each be related to the cartoon in contrasting ways. Source H provides a graphic visual description of impoverishment and squalor within the working class. On the one hand it might be seen as an indication that the working class was as yet too weak to inherit the earth. On the other hand, such conditions affected only a minority of the working class while the images of poverty and squalor provided a powerful incentive to press for workers' control. Source J is similarly ambivalent. It describes an overall improvement in the conditions of the German working class, perhaps reducing the need to 'inherit the earth'. At the same time, it draws attention to the concentration of workers in the cities, making their political organisation easier and more effective.

7

WAR AND COLLAPSE, 1914–18

BACKGROUND NARRATIVE

Germany entered the First World War in August 1914 with the expectation that the Schlieffen Plan would bring a swift victory. The intention was that the German armies would invade northern France via Belgium and win a rapid victory. This would enable German troops to be transferred to the eastern front to meet the anticipated Russian attack. The plan, however, was unsuccessful. The war on the western front became bogged down as the French held the advance in the Battle of the Marne (September 1914). The pattern of the war in the west changed from one of rapid campaigning to attrition in the trenches. The Battle of Verdun (1916) confirmed the stalemate, with the German forces unable to break through after early victories. A final attempt to end the deadlock was made in the middle of 1918. Again, little ground was won and the German war effort had been exhausted. The Reich suffered increasingly from the blockade of its ports by the Royal Navy, while the entry of the United States into the war in 1917 greatly increased the Allied strength during the course of 1918.

German armies were more successful on the eastern front. The Russian invasion was defeated in August 1914 at Tannenberg and the Masurian Lakes. From 1915 onwards, German forces penetrated deep into Russia and, following the revolutions of March and October 1917, Russia was forced to seek an armistice. The Treaty of

Brest Litovsk (March 1918) saw the transfer or independence of a swathe of territory from Finland to the Ukraine. Yet victory on the eastern front could not compensate for defeat in the west. Germany was therefore forced to sign an armistice on 11 November 1918.

The civilian experience of war changed dramatically between 1914 and 1918. The outbreak of war saw almost total consensus among the population that this was a just struggle. The absence of a swift victory, however, created widespread disillusionment. Civilian government under the Chancellors was overshadowed from 1917 by a virtual military dictatorship under Hindenburg and Ludendorff. This lasted until October 1918, when the prospect of defeat and the need for a quick armistice forced the Kaiser to replace the dictatorship with a constitutional government under the chancellorship of Prince Max of Baden. This, in turn, was replaced by a new republic, which was proclaimed from the Reichstag balcony on 9 November 1918. It was this government which signed the armistice and began the process of post-war reconstruction.

ANALYSIS (1): WHAT WERE GERMANY'S WAR AIMS AND WHY WERE THESE NOT ACHIEVED?

In the context of Germany and the First World War, the term 'aims' can be seen in three different ways.

The first 'aim' was related to Germany's actual involvement in war – the use of conflict to achieve domestic reconciliation. It has been argued by German historians such as Fischer that war provided the means whereby domestic reconciliation could be achieved between the different sectors of society. This, in turn, would relieve the pressure on the elites to reform a political system which still worked very much in their own favour. War would, in other words, channel the drive of the middle and working classes into patriotism rather than sectional interest. This meant that the SPD would lose its capacity to exert pressure for radical change and the whole impetus for democratisation would be reversed as the national interest would have to come first. Whether this was deliberate has already been discussed in Chapter 5. It seems unlikely that there was any conscious plan to seek the preservation of unity through the pursuit of war; but it is possible that the aggressive diplomacy followed by Germany up to August 1914 was based on a calculated risk and the attitude that the outbreak of war would be far from disastrous.

A more obvious 'aim' related to the outcome of the war. Clearly this involved victory; but for what purpose? Most Germans initially believed that they were involved in what was essentially a defensive war. Hence the object of victory was national survival. A substantial minority, however, had another expectation – territorial annexation and expansion. According to Fischer, Germany's official war aims, as put forward by the government, included: economic dominance over Belgium, Holland and France, hegemony over Courland, Livonia, Estonia, Lithuania and Poland in eastern Europe, and over Bulgaria, Romania and Turkey in the Balkans; unification with Austria and the creation of a Greater Germany; and the control over the entire eastern Mediterranean and over a dismantled Russia. There were also expectations of a greatly expanded overseas empire. This would include a broad band of territory across central Africa to link the existing colonies of German East Africa and South West Africa with territory to be taken from Britain and Belgium. The overall aim was the continuation of Weltpolitik outside Europe and Lebensraum inside. The extent to which this was intended at the beginning of the war is debatable. Fischer maintains that the emphasis of pre-war foreign policy had been expansionist and that war was the logical means whereby such a policy could be achieved. But it is equally arguable that Germany's territorial objectives came to be enlarged during the war itself.

The third 'aim' related to the actual conduct of the war: the search for a swift victory against an enemy coalition which had the strategic and numerical advantage. The problem was that Germany was confronted by the prospect of a war on two fronts, against France and Russia, who were both in the process of rapid rearmament. The solution was the Schlieffen Plan. This was based on the principle that the two enemies should be dealt with separately. This would involve a massive assault on France: the bulk of the German armies would pass rapidly through Belgium, sweep round to the west of Paris and trap the French and British against the 'anvil' of the remaining German forces in Alsace-Lorraine. The war in the west would be over within six weeks, enabling the bulk of the German troops to be transferred to the eastern front to combat the invading Russians. The German government and high command aimed to repeat the lightning strikes which had destroyed the military strength of France in 1870.

Germany therefore entered the First World War with the intention of rallying all social groups behind the Reich, in the expectation of victory and expansion which would, in turn, be achieved by the application of a systematic plan of campaign. Just over four years later Germany experienced both defeat and internal chaos. What went wrong? In reverse order, all three of the aims remained unachieved.

The Schlieffen Plan did not work as intended, with the result that there was no ultimate victory and social divisions were exacerbated rather than healed. There were several reasons for the failure of the Schlieffen Plan. The details were modified at the last minute; they were, for example, reworked so as to avoid sending troops through Holland. This meant that the invasion was concentrated on a narrower front and was therefore easier for the French and British to contain. To make matters worse, part of the forces originally allocated to the attack through Belgium were used to reinforce the holding army in Alsace-Lorraine. There was also an unevenness in technology which undermined the German invasion. It was possible to get large numbers of troops by railway to the designated points on the frontier; thereafter, however, the more traditional forced march was too slow to achieve a breakthrough against the enemy defences. There was, at this stage, no means of countering the trench and its accompaniment – barbed wire. It was not until the development of the tank that a fully mechanised invasion was possible beyond the railheads. In 1914, therefore, the initiative was inevitably with the defender rather than with the attacker. The advantage was not reversed until 1940, which saw the use of the more mobile panzer divisions. In the meantime, the French and British had the psychological as well as the military advantage because they were more effectively geared to a protracted war of attrition as their ultimate success did not depend on immediate victory in any specific sector.

Ironically, Germany achieved its greatest success in the area which was initially of the lower priority. From the time of the Battle of Tannenberg in 1914, the Russian armies were comprehensively defeated and the Germans were able to inflict the Treaty of Brest Litovsk in March 1918. This went some way towards achieving the aim of expansion in the east. Yet, without a corresponding victory in the west, this success counted for nothing. The conquest of substantial parts of Russia did not mean the automatic transfer of German troops from the eastern to the western front. Even after the Treaty of Brest Litovsk almost as many troops were needed to occupy the areas as it had taken to conquer them in the first place. Those troops who were released did, it is true, make possible a new offensive against the west in March 1918 but this was only temporarily successful and the German advance was confined to a distance of forty miles. In the process, German armies expended all their energy and resources and were unable to sustain the impetus or meet the eventual counter-attack.

German troops were also required to assist Austria-Hungary. Even though the Russian threat was removed, the Habsburg Empire faced in 1918 problems of internal revolt from its Slav population – from the Serbs and Croats in the south and the Czechs and Slovaks in the north.

Stalemate in France eventually served to widen the scope of the war in the west. This was the reverse of the original German strategy of a rapid victory there before aiming at expansion in the east. The longer the struggle lasted the more likely it was that the Royal Navy would be able to play a decisive role. The Battle of Jutland convinced the High Command that Germany could not hope to win future naval engagements against Britain; hence the German surface fleet was confined to port for the rest of the war. This had two effects, both of which severely damaged Germany's war effort and reduced the chances of German victory. One was that the Royal Navy was able to place a blockade around the German coastline and starve the German economy and people of essential supplies of raw materials and food. The other was the resort by Germany to submarine warfare. This was a measure of desperation, intended to compensate for Germany's failure to control the seas. But there were serious repercussions. Germany's blockade was very different to that of Britain in that it involved the indiscriminate sinking of merchant shipping. This failed to bring about the anticipated collapse of the British economy. Worse still, it widened the scope of the war to include the United States, which suffered particularly severely from Germany's submarine campaign. According to Berghahn: 'No other German policy in the First World War did more to bring the Americans into the war, yet fail to force Britain to her knees.' (1)

The arrival of over 1 million American servicemen in France made possible a sustained counter-attack of the Allies in August 1918. There was also the possibility of an Allied invasion of Alsace-Lorraine while the collapse of the Ottoman Empire, Bulgaria and Austria-Hungary laid open the south and east to the Allies. With the real prospect of defeat came the hard reality facing the High Command that concessions would have to be made in the search for a negotiated settlement. This, in turn, set in motion a train of events which resulted eventually in a political revolution as the accompaniment to military defeat. The Second Reich ended on 9 November 1918, two days before the surrender of Germany.

Questions

1. Were the German people agreed on the reasons for the outbreak of the war and on the type of victory to be achieved?

2. Why was defeat in the west eventually to prove more important for Germany than victory in the east?

ANALYSIS (2): WHAT EFFECT DID THE FIRST WORLD WAR HAVE ON GERMANY?

The First World War had a varied impact on Germany and the German people. Initially it helped rally and unite the different sections of the population. In the longer term, however, it threw into even sharper relief the divisions which had always existed between them.

One of the notable features of the first year of the war was the extent of its popularity. This applied to all the major participants, especially to Germany. Part of the reason was a strong belief that Germany was involved in a defensive war which was not of its making. Hence there was a political truce between the various parties and interests, known as the 'Burgfriede'. Most of the groups within the population seemed to benefit from this. The elites had the means of diverting attention away from domestic issues into a patriotic and nationalist crusade; according to Fischer and others, this is what they had always intended. If anything, it worked better than they had anticipated. The ruling class had been expecting to have to take action against the working-class organisations which, they thought, would inevitably oppose the war. In fact, the reverse was the case. For even the left was caught up in the fervour of patriotism. Most of the SPD supported the war effort, partly through an underlying patriotism and partly in the belief that war would bring with it a recognition from the rest of society of the true worth of the working class. The middle classes were similarly enthusiastic. Even the liberal historian Meinecke welcomed the conflict, believing that it would achieve what had not been possible during the long period of peace since 1871 – the full integration of Prussia into Germany and the creation of a people's army. Paradoxically, therefore, war would have a liberalising effect. This was described by Meinecke as the 'inner Sedan', a means of completing the process of unification which the Franco-Prussian War had started.

The majority of the population therefore believed that Germany was involved in a 'just' war. This meant that its participation was primarily defensive. Only the radical wing of the SPD opposed the war in principle. But even here there was a strong feeling that war would serve the purpose of revolution by destabilising the regime. Ultimately this proved to be correct. The first two years, it is true, saw a political truce and a strong sense of common purpose and identity. Gradually, however, this was undermined, resulting in creeping dictatorship and growing divisions within the different sectors of the population.

The thought of war was beneficial; the prolonged experience of war was destructive. The losses for Germany were particularly heavy. Something like 2.4 million people were killed, with even more wounded or permanently disabled. The shortage of food and imports became especially serious in 1917. This was partly because of the growing success of the British naval blockade and partly because of a cold winter in 1916–17 and a bad harvest in the summer of 1917. In 1918 alone, civilian deaths from starvation and disease totalled 293,000. The German economy was dislocated through its deprivation of vital imports of raw materials and food. There was no alternative but to undergo total mobilisation to enable the military to try to break through the strategic stalemate on the western front.

At first this was confined to the economic sector, with the establishment of the Raw Materials Department, or KRA. This had responsibility for the distribution of key raw materials to where they were most needed. The War Ministry supplemented this with measures for the conscription of labour. Gradually, however, the war effort came to encompass the political sector as well. The military crisis, brought on by the failure to break through on the western front, saw a fundamental change in the political system within Germany. The Chancellor, Bethmann Hollweg, found it necessary, because of the unsatisfactory conduct of the war, to replace Falkenhayn as commander-in-chief by Hindenburg, who had already been successful in defeating the Russians on the eastern front. This move, however, transformed the political system. The Kaiser, so influential before 1914, now ceased to function effectively as head of state. The Chancellor also became subordinate in effect to the military High Command – or Oberste Heeresleitung (OHL). In June 1917 Bethmann Hollweg resigned and although the fiction of civilian government was officially maintained, the real ruling force was the army.

Economic mobilisation was intended to lay the foundations of victory. But political dictatorship was a sign that this was not going to happen. The various groups within the population became disillusioned. The elites found that war without swift victory brought internal dissension rather than external diversion. The middle and lower classes found that military crisis brought the very opposite of the democracy they sought. It was not so much that Germany stood out among the combatants in turning to authoritarian rule: Britain and France also experienced a greater degree of centralisation in 1918 than they had in 1914. However, Britain and France remained in essence democracies which temporarily operated a state of emergency while Lloyd George and Clemenceau maintained full civilian control over the military. In Germany the problem was that the army had ultimate control over the civilian sector which had largely ceased to function on pre-war lines.

All this meant the gradual breaking of the consensus which had emerged in 1914. By August 1918 the situation in Germany was desperate. The prolonged war acted as a catalyst for the decomposition of consensus into the constituent parts. Politics once again polarised, becoming potentially more confrontational as a result of impending military defeat. The middle classes again became suspicious of the regime which now had a narrower base than ever before. The left was again radicalised, and there was a recurrence of the split between evolutionists and revolutionaries. They had in common their dislike of military dictatorship, although they differed as to what its replacement should be. Even the decision of the OHL to hand over power to a civilian government in October 1918 failed to prevent the re-emergence of the social divisions of pre-war Germany. The reason for this is that the transfer of power was necessitated by the need for an armistice, which the Allies refused to negotiate with Hindenburg's dictatorship. Prince Max of Baden's constitutional government was soon overtaken on the left by the proclamation of a republic on 9 November by the SPD. This, in turn, was challenged by the radical left in the form of the Spartacists.

By the end of the war hardly any of the original political parties remained intact. The war might be said to have been a period of turmoil which had transformed the social structure and the political spectrum which overlay it. In fact, the reverse is true. The parties which had emerged by 1919 were in large part a sharpening of the old divisions and attitudes. The Conservatives were replaced by the more strident Nationalists. The split between the National Liberals and the Progressives was now re-enacted by that between the People's Party and the Democrats. The socialist left fragmented into three parts: the majority Social Democrats and the more radical Spartacists and Independent Socialists: the last two eventually merged to form the Communist Party. The real situation was that the war brought defeat to Germany which, in turn, toppled the regime that had initiated it: in this respect it was a catalyst for progressive constitutional change in the form of the Weimar Republic. However, the experience of defeat sharpened existing social antagonisms with the result that the new government had to coexist with an exceptionally wide range of political parties.

To summarise the overall argument of this section, the outbreak of war brought an unexpected degree of unity amongst most of the sections of German society. This was fostered by the belief that Germany was the victim of external aggression and that the war would soon result in victory over the aggressors. When this failed to materialise the fault lines in German society reopened under the pressure of economic privation which was due to the success of the British blockade on Germany's ports. The military dictatorship of Hindenburg and Ludendorff failed to pull Germany together and had to give way to a more constitutional alternative. This, in turn, gave way to a revolution from below and the replacement of the Second Reich by the Weimar Republic. From its inception, however, the republic faced a heightened form of all the internal tensions of the Reich.

Questions

1. Why did the outbreak of war unite the German people?
2. Did the pursuit of the war divide the German people?

SOURCES

ATTITUDES IN GERMANY TO THE FIRST WORLD WAR

Source A: the view of the German historian, Friedrich Meinecke, in 1914.

Industrial Germany, with all the mass that it encompasses, has shown its will and its might ... At the same time the unfortunate tensions that existed between the conservative forces of Prussia and the liberal needs of wider Germany have diminished ... If our army succeeds in bringing about a full synthesis of people's army and professional army, then in the life of our state the full synthesis of Prussian organism and Reich organism can also come about.

Source B: proclamation of Wilhelm II, 6 August 1914.

To the German People.
Ever since the foundation of our empire it has been the greatest endeavour for me and for my forefathers over the last 43 years to preserve peace in the world and to continue our powerful development in peace. But our enemies envy the success of our work ... now these enemies want to humiliate us. They wish us to look on with folded arms as they prepare a malicious attack; they do not tolerate our standing side by side in determined loyalty with our allies ...

Therefore the sword must now decide. In the midst of peace the enemy attacks us. Forward. To arms. Every moment of wavering, every hesitation is treason against the Fatherland. The existence or destruction of our recreated empire is now at stake, the very existence of German power and customs. We will resist to the last breath of air of man and horse. And we will win this fight even against a world of enemies. Germany has never lost when it has been united. Forward with God who will be with us as He was with our fathers.

Source C: from a letter from Friedrich Meinecke to a friend, 21 October 1918.

A fearful and gloomy existence awaits us in the best of circumstances! And although my hatred of the enemy, who remind me of beasts of prey, is as hot as ever, so is my anger and resentment at those power politicians who, by their presumption and their stupidity, have dragged us down into this abyss. Repeatedly in the course of the war, we could have had a peace by agreement, if it had not been that boundless demands of the Pan-German–militaristic–conservative combine could be broken only by the overthrow of the whole state.

Source D: from a speech delivered by Philipp Scheidemann, a leader of the SPD, from the Reichstag balcony to the crowd below, 9 November 1918.

Workers and soldiers, frightful were those four years of war, ghastly the sacrifices the people made in blood and treasure. The cursed War is at an end. Murder has ceased. The fruits of war, want and misery, will burden us for years. The catastrophe we tried our best to avoid has not been spared us . . . The foes of an industrious people, the real foes in our midst, that have caused Germany's downfall, are silent and invisible. These were the warriors who stopped at home, promoting their demands for annexation, bitterly opposing any reform of the constitution . . . These foes are, it is to be hoped, gone for good. The Emperor has abdicated. He and his friends have decamped. The people have triumphed over them all along the line . . . The old and rotten – the monarchy – has broken down. Long live the new! Long live the German Republic!

Source E: extracts from the testimony of Field Marshal von Hindenburg to the investigative committee on the war, November 1919.

The concern as to whether the homeland would remain resolute until the war was won, from this moment on, never left us. We often raised a warning voice to the Reich government. At this time, the secret intentional mutilation of the fleet and the army began as a continuation of similar occurrences in peace time . . . The obedient troops who remained immune to revolutionary attrition suffered greatly from the behaviour, in violation of duty, of their revolutionary comrades; they had to carry the battle the whole time ... The intentions of the command could no longer be executed. Our repeated proposals for strict discipline and strict legislation were not adopted. Thus did our operations necessarily miscarry; the collapse was inevitable; the revolution provided the keystone ... An English general said with justice: 'The German army was stabbed in the back.'

Questions

1. (i) Explain the references to the 'Pan-German–militaristic–conservative combine' (Source C). (2 marks)
   (ii) What position was held by Field Marshal von Hindenburg (Source E) between 1917 and 1918? (1 mark)
2. In what ways is Source C (a) consistent and (b) inconsistent with Source A? (4 marks)
3. How effectively is language and tone used in Source B to put across its message? (4 marks)
4. How do Sources D and E differ in their view of the enemies of Germany? How would you explain these differences? (6 marks)
5. 'The mood of the German people to the war was radically different in 1918 to what it had been in 1914.' To what extent do these sources, and your own knowledge, suggest that this view is correct? (8 marks)

NOTES

1. THE FORMATION AND STRUCTURE OF THE GERMAN EMPIRE

1 C. Grant Robertson: *Bismarck* (London 1918), p. 128.
2 Quoted in W. Carr: *A History of Germany 1815–1945* (London 1969), ch. 4.
3 A.J.P. Taylor: *Bismarck. The Man and the Statesman* (London 1961), p. 162.
4 Quoted in ibid., ch. IV.
5 H. Bohme (ed.): *The Foundations of the German Empire. Select Documents*, trans. by A. Ramm, Document 69.
6 Quoted in F.B.M. Hollyday (ed.): *Bismarck*, Part I.
7 J.M. Keynes: *The Economic Consequences of the Peace* (London 1919), p. 75.
8 Quoted in G. Eley: 'Bismarckian Germany', in G. Martel (ed.): *Modern Germany Reconsidered 1870–1945* (London 1992), p. 2.
9 F.B.M. Hollyday: op. cit., Part I.
10 W.J. Mommsen: *Imperial Germany 1867–1918* (London 1995), p. 1.
11 Ibid., p. 5.
12 Quoted in ibid., p. 22.
Source A: Quoted in G. Craig: *The Politics of the Prussian Army, 1640–1945* (Oxford 1955), p. 160.
Source B: W.N. Medlicott and D.K. Coveney (eds): *Bismarck and Europe* (London 1971), p. 31.
Source C: quoted in J.C.G. Röhl (ed.): *From Bismarck to Hitler. The Problem of Continuity in German History* (London 1970), pp. 20–21.
Source D: *Memoirs and Letters of Sir Robert Morier* (London 1911), Vol. ii, pp. 71–72.

Source E: quoted in T.S. Hamerow (ed.): *Otto von Bismarck: A Historical Assessment* (Boston, Mass. 1966), p. 18.

Source F: P. Pulzer: *Germany 1870–1945* (Oxford 1997), p. 16.

Source G: W.M. Simon: *Germany in the Age of Bismarck* (London 1968), p. 154.

Source H: Ibid., p. 153.

Source I: *Germany in the Age of Bismarck*, (London 1968), p. 121.

Source J: *Germany in the Age of Bismarck*, (London 1968), p. 153.

2. DOMESTIC POLICIES, 1871–90

1 G.A. Craig: *Germany 1866–1945* (Oxford 1978), ch. V.
2 W.M. Simon: *Germany in the Age of Bismarck* (London 1968), Document 39.
3 W.J. Mommsen: op. cit., p. 59.
Source A: W.M. Simon: op. cit., p. 132.
Source B: ibid., p. 148.
Source C: A.J.P. Taylor: op. cit., p. 138.
Source D: G.E. Buckle (ed.): *The Letters of Queen Victoria*, vol. 3 (London 1930), pp. 169–70.
Source E: W.M. Simon: op. cit., pp. 170–71.
Source F: ibid., pp. 170–71.
Source G: ibid., p. 164.

3. FOREIGN AND COLONIAL POLICIES, 1871–90

1 W.L. Langer: *European Alliances and Alignments, 1871–1890* (New York 1931), pp. 503–04.
2 H. Holborn: *A History of Modern Germany, Vol. 3: 1840–1945* (London 1969), Ch. 6.
3 A.J.P. Taylor: op. cit., p. 189.
4 Quoted in M.E. Townsend: *The Rise and Fall of Germany's Colonial Empire* (New York 1930), p. 160.
5 Quoted in E. Eyck: *Bismarck and the German Empire* (London 1958), p. 272.
6 M.E. Townsend: op. cit., p. 6.
7 J.K. Walton: *Disraeli* (London 1990), ch. 4.
8 D. Thomson: *Europe since Napoleon* (London 1957), ch. 20.
9 D.K. Fieldhouse, 'Imperialism; an Historiographical Revision', *Economic History Review*, xiv.
10 V.R. Berghahn: *Imperial Germany 1871–1914: Economy, Society, Culture and Politics* (Oxford 1994), p. 266.
11 A.J.P. Taylor: *The Struggle for Mastery in Europe 1848–1918* (Oxford 1954), ch. XIII.

12 W.L. Langer: op. cit., ch. IX.
13 A.J.P. Taylor: *Germany's First Bid For Colonies, 1884–1885* (London), p. 6.
14 D.G. Williamson: *Bismarck and Germany 1862–1890* (Harlow 1986), p. 79.
15 V.R. Berghahn: op. cit., p. 266.
16 Quoted in E. Eyck: op. cit., p. 275.
Source A: M. Hurst (ed.): *Key Treaties for the Great Powers 1814–1914* (Newton Abbot 1972), vol. 2, p. 590.
Source B: ibid., p. 646.
Source C: W.N. Medlicott and D.K Coveney: op. cit., p. 166.
Source D: T.S. Hamerow (ed.): *The Age of Bismarck. Documents and Interpretations* (London 1973), pp. 142–43.
Source E: W.N. Medlicott and D.K. Coveney: op. cit., p. 138.
Source F: W.L. Langer: op. cit., ch. IX.
Source G: W.N. Medlicott and D.K. Coveney: op. cit., p. 142.
Source H: quoted in A.J.P. Taylor: *Bismarck*, op. cit., p. 216.

4. DOMESTIC POLICIES, 1890–1914

1 W.J. Mommsen: op. cit., p. 53.
2 See J.C.G. Röhl: *Germany without Bismarck: The Crisis of Government in the Second Reich, 1890–1900* (London 1967).
3 Quoted in K.A. Lerman: *Kaiser Wilhelm II: Last Emperor of Imperial Germany* (in *Modern History Review*, April 1990).
4 P. Pulzer: op. cit., p. 57.
5 See F. Fischer: *Germany's Aims in the First World War* (London 1967; originally published 1961) and *War of Illusions: German Policies 1911–1914* (New York 1975; originally published 1969).
6 See H.-U. Wehler: *The German Empire 1871–1918* (Leamington Spa 1985; originally published 1973).
7 Ibid., p. 64.
8 J. Retallack: 'Wilhelmine Germany', in G. Martel (ed.): *Modern Germany Reconsidered 1870–1945* (London 1992), p. 44.
9 R.J. Evans (ed.): *Society and Politics in Wilhelmine Germany* (London 1978), p. 28.
10 See D. Blackbourn: 'The Problem of Democratisation: German Catholics and the Role of the Centre Party', in R.J. Evans: op. cit.
11 See E. Kehr: *Battleship Building and Party Politics in Germany* (Chicago 1973).
Source A: quoted in J.A. Nichols: *Germany after Bismarck. The Caprivi Era 1890–1894* (Cambridge, Mass. 1958), p. 71.
Source B: quoted in ibid., p. 338.

Source C: quoted in ibid., p. 341.

Source D: W. Carr: op. cit.

Source E: A. Fried and R. Sanders (eds): *Socialist Thought* (London 1964).

Source F: T.A. Kohut: *Wilhelm II and the Germans: A Study in Leadership* (Oxford 1991), pp. 228–29.

Source G: M. Balfour: *The Kaiser and his Times* (London 1964), p. 158.

Source H: quoted in G. Layton: *From Bismarck to Hitler: Germany 1890–1933* (London 1995), p. 16.

Source I: T.A. Kohut: op. cit., p. 173.

Source J: J.C.G. Röhl: *Germany without Bismarck*, op. cit., p. 279.

Source K: *Sigmund Freud: New Introductory Lectures on Psycho-analysis* (Harmondsworth 1979), p. 97.

Source L: quoted in J.C.G. Röhl: *The Kaiser*, op. cit., p. 110.

5. FOREIGN AND IMPERIAL POLICIES, 1890–1914

1 Quoted in P. Pulzer: op. cit., p. 73.
2 H.H. Herwig: *Hammer or Anvil? Modern Germany 1648–Present* (Lexington, Mass. 1994), p. 180.
3 G. Layton: op. cit., p. 32.
4 K.A. Lerman: 'Kaiser Wilhelm II', *Modern History Review*, April 1990, p. 4.
5 K.S. Pinson: *Modern Germany* (New York 1954), ch. XII.
6 V.R. Berghahn: *Germany and the Approach of War in 1914* (London 1973), Ch. 2.
7 Quoted in G.A. Craig: *Germany*, op. cit., ch. VII.
8 Quoted in V.R. Berghahn: *Germany*, op. cit., ch. 2.
9 H.-U. Wehler: op. cit., pp. 176–77.
10 Report presented to the Preliminary Peace Conference 1919, in D.E. Lee (ed.): *The Outbreak of the First World War* (Boston, Mass. 1968).
11 Quoted in G.A. Craig: *Germany*, op. cit., Ch. IX.
12 Quoted in L.F.C. Turner: *Origins of the First World War* (London 1970), ch. 4.
13 Quoted in P. Pulzer: op. cit., p. 78.

Source A: quoted in J.A. Nichols: op. cit., p. 113.

Source B: quoted in ibid., p. 113.

Source C: M. Hurst: op. cit., document 141.

Source D: quoted in T.A. Kohut: op. cit., p. 187.

Source E: quoted in J.C.G. Röhl: *The Kaiser*, op. cit., p. 180.

Source F: V.R. Berghahn and M. Kitchen (eds): *Germany in the Age of Total War* (London 1981), p. 41.

Source G: ibid.

Source H: G. Martel: *The Origins of the First World War* (Harlow 1987), document 11.

Source I: ibid., document 12.

6. ECONOMY AND SOCIETY, 1871–1914

1 W.J. Mommsen: op. cit., p. 103.
2 V.R. Berghahn: *Imperial Germany*, op. cit., p. 11.
3 Ibid., p. 42.
4 P. Pulzer: op. cit., p. 49.
5 V.R. Berghahn: *Imperial Germany*, op. cit., pp. 30–31.

Source A: adapted from D.G. Williamson: op. cit., p. 103.

Source B: adapted from P. Pulzer: op. cit., p. 47.

Source C: adapted from V.R. Berghahn: *Modern Germany*, op. cit., p. 279.

Source D: adapted from ibid.

Source E: adapted from ibid., p. 298.

Source F: adapted from D.G. Williamson: op. cit., p. 108.

Source G: quoted in V.R. Berghahn: *Modern Germany*, op. cit., p. 7.

Source H: from Archiv für Kunst und Geschichte, London, and published in D. Blackbourn: *The Fontana History of Germany 1780–1918* (London 1997).

Source I: from *Der wahre Jakob* and published in D. Blackbourn: *The Fontana History of Germany 1780–1918* (London 1997).

Source J: quoted in T.S. Hamerow (ed.): *The Age of Bismarck*, op. cit.

Source K: quoted in S. Miller: *Mastering Modern European History* (London 1997), p. 233.

7. WAR AND COLLAPSE, 1914–18

1 V.R. Berghahn: *Modern Germany*, op. cit., p. 46.

Source A: quoted in P. Pulzer: op. cit., p. 81.

Source B: quoted in G. Layton: op. cit., p. 58.

Source C: quoted in ibid., p. 72.

Source D: quoted in L.L. Snyder: *The Weimar Republic* (Princeton, NJ 1966), Reading No. 3.

Source E: quoted in A. Kaes, M. Jay and E. Dimendberg: *The Weimar Republic Sourcebook* (Berkeley 1994), pp. 15–16.

BIBLIOGRAPHY

This brief survey includes the main works referred to in compiling this book. They are all readily accessible. Some appear several times since they are appropriate to the periods 1871–1914, 1871–90 and 1890–1914.

PRIMARY SOURCES

The following books provide a selection of documentary extracts which have been translated into English: H. Bohme (ed.): *The Foundations of the German Empire. Select Documents*, trans. by A. Ramm; D.G. Williamson: *Bismarck and Germany 1862–1890* (Harlow 1986); T.S. Hamerow (ed.): *The Age of Bismarck. Documents and Interpretations* (London 1973); W.M. Simon: *Germany in the Age of Bismarck* (London 1968); W.N. Medlicott and D.K. Coveney (eds): *Bismarck and Europe* (London 1971); and M. Hurst (ed.): *Key Treaties for the Great Powers 1814–1914* (Newton Abbot 1972), 2 vols.

SECONDARY SOURCES

There are several very comprehensive general works on modern Germany. Three of these provide a detailed and traditional approach. These are H. Holborn: *A History of Modern Germany, Vol. 3: 1840–1945* (London 1969); W. Carr: *A History of Germany 1815–1945* (London 1969); and G.A. Craig: *Germany 1866–1945* (Oxford 1978). Others, containing some stimulating revisionist views, are P. Pulzer: *Germany 1870–1945* (Oxford 1997); W.J. Mommsen: *Imperial Germany 1867–1918* (London 1995); J.C.G. Röhl (ed.): *From Bismarck to Hitler. The Problem of Continuity in German History* (London 1970); G. Martel (ed.): *Modern Germany Reconsidered 1870–1945* (London 1992); V.R. Berghahn: *Imperial Germany, 1871–1914* (Providence, RI, and Oxford 1994); and H.-U. Wehler: *The German Empire 1871–1918* (Leamington Spa 1985; originally published 1973).

Approaches to Bismarck vary widely. The more traditional are C. Grant Robertson: *Bismarck* (London 1918); and E. Eyck: *Bismarck and the German Empire* (London 1958). The first major revisionist line was taken in A.J.P. Taylor: *Bismarck. The Man and the Statesman* (London 1961). Since then there has been a wide range of interpretations, contained in G. Martel (ed.): *Modern Germany Reconsidered 1870–1945* (London 1992); V.R. Berghahn: *Imperial Germany, 1871–1914* (Providence, RI, and Oxford 1994); H.-U. Wehler: *The German Empire 1871–1918* (Leamington Spa 1985; originally published 1973); and T.S. Hamerow (ed.): *Otto von Bismarck: A Historical Assessment* (Boston 1966).

A good, if brief, introduction to the Wilhelmine period is G. Layton: *From Bismarck to Hitler: Germany 1890–1933* (London 1995). More detailed are G.M. Balfour: *The Kaiser and his Times* (London 1964); J.C.G. Röhl: *The Kaiser and his Court* (Cambridge 1994); I. Porter and I.D. Armour: *Imperial Germany 1890–1918* (Harlow 1991); J.C.G. Röhl: *Germany without Bismarck: The Crisis of Government in the Second Reich, 1890–1900* (London 1967); J.A. Nichols: *Germany after Bismarck. The Caprivi Era 1890–1894* (Cambridge, Mass. 1958); T.A. Kohut: *Wilhelm II and the Germans: A Study in Leadership* (Oxford 1991); F. Fischer: *Germany's Aims in the First World War* (London 1967); V.R. Berghahn: *Germany and the Approach of War in 1914* (London 1973); D.E. Lee (ed.): *The Outbreak of the First World War* (Lexington, Mass. 1963); L.F.C. Turner: *Origins of the First World War* (London 1970); G. Martel: *The Origins of the First World War* (Harlow 1987); F. Fischer: *War of Illusions: German Policies 1911–1914* (New York 1975); and R.J. Evans (ed.): *Society and Politics in Wilhelmine Germany* (London 1978). In addition, the following titles, already cited, are again relevant: P. Pulzer: *Germany 1870–1945* (Oxford

1997); W.J. Mommsen: *Imperial Germany 1867–1918* (London 1995); J.C.G. Röhl (ed.): *From Bismarck to Hitler. The Problem of Continuity in German History* (London 1970); G. Martel (ed.): *Modern Germany Reconsidered 1870–1945* (London 1992); V.R. Berghahn: *Imperial Germany, 1871–1914* (Providence, RI, and Oxford 1994); and H.-U. Wehler: *The German Empire 1871–1918* (Leamington Spa 1985; originally published 1973).

INDEX

Note: Page numbers in **Bold** *refer to Background Narratives*

Africa, German colonies in *38*, 44, 45, 46, 47, 75, 107
Agadir crisis (1911) **73**, 75, 83
Agrarian League 63
agricultural interests 23, 28, 29–30, **54**, **55**, 63, 82
agriculture 91, 92, 95
Alexander II, Tsar 41
Algeçiras Conference (1906) **73**, 75
Allgemeine Elektrizitts-Gesellschaft (AEG) 93
Allied Commission on War Guilt 81
Allies **105**
Alsace **3**, 21, 39, 41, 45, 46, **55**, 57
Alsace-Lorraine 39, 41, 45, 46, 107, 109
Andrássy 41
Anglo-French Entente (1904) **38**, **72–3**, 75, 83
Anglo-German Agreement on East Africa (1886) 46
Anglo-German Agreement on Portugal's colonies (1898) **72**
Anglo-German China Agreement (1900) **72**
Anglo-Russian Convention (1907) **38**, **73**, 75, 83
anti-semitism 78
anti-socialist laws **19**, 22–3, 25, 26, 29, **54**, 58, 96; attempt by Hohenlohe to renew 63; Wilhelm II refuses to renew 43
armistice (1918) **106**
army, Prussian **2**; under Wilhelm II 57, 64, 78; Wilhelm II's speech to recruits (1891) 68; *see also* military dictatorship
Army Bill (1887) 24, 43
Austria **1**, **2**, 5, 21, 22, 42, 43, 74, 81, 82; alliance with (1864) 6; Hitler annexes (1939) 85; Prussian war with (1866) **2–3**, 4, **37**; smaller German states' support for 6–7; sources on 12–14; in Triple Alliance **38**, 39, 40, 41
Austria-Hungary **37–8**, 63, 75, 85, 109; Ausgleich (1867) 27; declares war on Russia (1914) **74**; declares war on Serbia (1914) **73**; *see also* Dual Alliance (1879)
Austrian Ambassador in Berlin, report to Foreign Minister of Austria-Hungary (1914) 89
Austrian Empire **1**
Austrian Succession, War of the (1740–48) 84
authoritarianism 9–12, 57–8, 96

Baden **3**, 6, 7, 10
Badische Presse, Die 68

Baghdad–Berlin rail link proposal
72
Balkan Wars (1912–13) 81, 83
Balkans 63, **72**, **73**, 76, 80, 82;
    crisis (1875–78) **37**, 40;
    crisis (1885–87) **38**, 39, 41
Bamberger, Ludwig 20; *Herr von
    Bismarck* extract 31
banking 93
Basserman 88
Bavaria **3**, 6, 7, 10, 16, 22, 30
Bayer 92
Bebel, August 66
Belgium 4, 5, 27, **73**, 82, 84, 85,
    105, 107, 108; industrialisa-
    tion 91, 92
Berghahn, V.R. 45, 47, 74, 83, 92,
    93, 96, 109
Berlin 95; Congress of (1878) **37**,
    40, 74; photograph of slum
    (1905) 101; uprising (1848)
    1
Berlin Conference (1884–85) 46,
    74
Berlin–Baghdad rail link proposal
    72
Bernstein, Eduard 66–7
Bessemer process 8
Bethmann Hollweg, Theobald von
    (1909–17) **54**, **55**, 62, 78,
    83, 84–5, 111
Bismarck, Herbert (son) 47, 52
Bismarck, Otto von 56; alliances
    37–48, sources 49–50;
    authoritarianism of 9–12,
    31–2; colonial policy, sources
    51–2; conversation with
    British Ambassador in Berlin
    51; description by Lady Emily
    Russell 31–2; domestic
    policies (1871–90) **18–19**,
    20–6, 30; foreign and colonial
    policies (1871–90) **37–8**,
    39–43, 44–8, 84; and
    Franco-Prussian war **3**; as
    Imperial Chancellor
    (1871–90) **3**, **18**; influences
    on later foreign policy 74–7,
    86–7; letter to Bray, Prime
    Minister of Bavaria (1870) 16;

letter to Lord Salisbury (1887)
    49–50; letter to Otto
    Manteuffel 12–13; Memoirs
    13; Minister President of
    Prussia (1862) **2**, **3**; relations
    with Kaisers 24, 61; report to
    Wilhelm I (1871) 15–16;
    resignation (1890) **19**, 25, **38**,
    54, 56, 61, **71**; role in
    unification 4, 5–8, 30; speech
    to Prussian Landtag (1862)
    13; speech to Prussian upper
    chamber (1873) 33; speech
    to Reichstag (1881) 31;
    speech to the Reichstag
    Budget Commission (1884)
    52; telegram from Wilhelm I
    of Prussia which he rewrote
    (1870) **3**; to the French
    Ambassador (1885) 52
Björkö Agreement (1905) **73**, 77
Blackbourn, D. 59, 60
Bleichröder, Gerson 100
Blue-Black Bloc 62
Bochum 59–60
Boers **72**
Bohemia **1**; Hitler annexes (1939)
    85
Böhme, H. 8, 28
Boldt 12
Bonapartism 12
Bosnia-Herzegovina **73**, 75, 83
Bosnian Serbs **73**
Bray, Prime Minister of Bavaria,
    letter from Bismarck to (1870)
    16
Brest Litovsk, Treaty of (1918)
    106, 108
Britain 24, **38**, 44, 75, 91,
    111–12; colonies 46, 47;
    Conservative Party 45; and
    the *Daily Telegraph* Affair
    (1908) **55**, 57–8, 65, 79;
    declares war on Germany
    (1914) **73–4**; Germany's
    relations with 57–8, **72**, 75,
    76–7; industrialisation 91, 92;
    Liberal Unionists 27; naval
    blockade **105**, 109, 111, 113;
    and the navy 64, 79; Reform

Act (1867) 27; role in outbreak of WWI 81; social reforms 63; splendid isolation of **72**

British Ambassador in Berlin, conversation with Bismarck 51

British Royal Commission on labour conditions in Central Europe (1893) 102–3

Bulgaria 82, 107, 109; crisis (1885) **38**, 40, 41

Bulgarians 37

Bull of Papal Infallibility 21

Bülow, Bernhard, Fürst von (1900–09) **54–5**, 56–7, 61–3, 64, 78, 79; on foreign policy 80

Bülow bloc 62

Bundesrat 10

'Burgfriede' 110

Bussman 9

calculated risk thesis 83, 106

capitalism 96

Caprivi, Georg Leo von, (1890–94) 42, **54**, 56, 61, 64, 76, 78, 79; 'New Course' **54**, 58, 59, 62–3, 65, 79; newspaper comment on 86; speech to the Reichstag (1891) 103; telegram from Kaiser to 66

cartels, industrial 93–4, 96

Catholic Church, Bismarck and the see Kulturkampf

Catholicism 7, 60

Centre Party 11, **18**, 21, 22, 26, 27, **54**, **55**, 60, 62, 79; Bismarck courts 23–4, 25, 30, 43; seats in Reichstag (1871–90) 34; support for navy 64, 78

Chancellors **3**, **54**; and the Reichstag 61, 62; relations with Kaiser 61

Charlemagne 1

chemical industry 92

China **72**

Christian IX of Denmark **2**

Clausewitz, Karl von, on war 78–9, 84

Clemenceau, Georges 112

coal and steel industry 8, 91, 92, 98

Cologne 95

colonialism 24, 44–8, **55**, 64, 65, 75

colonies **38**

commercial regulations, German states **18**, 20

commercial treaties 63, 103

Commerz-und-Disconto Bank 93

Communist Party 97, 112

Congo 46

Congolese Treaty, Britain's **72**

conscription 111

conservatism, and imperialism 48

Conservative Party 11, 23, 24, 25, **54**, 62, 65, 80, 96, 112; Prussian Junker-based **19**, 20–1, 29

Constitution (1851) 57

Constitution (1871) 20, 27, 29, 56, 61; sources 15–16

constitutional government **106**

Courland 82, 107

Crimean War (1854–56) 5

criminal code **18**, 20

cultural unity 1

culture struggle see Kulturkampf

currency, common **18**, 20

customs union see Zollverein

Daily Telegraph Affair (1908) **55**, 57–8, 65, 79

Danubian customs union 8

defence policy 64, 74

Delbrück 8

Democrats 112

Denmark 2; war with (1864) 4, **37**

Deutsche Bank 93

dictatorship, military **106**, 111–12, 113

Diet of German Confederation 1, 6, 10

diplomacy 39–48, **71–3**, 75

Diplomatic Revolution (1755–56) 84

Disraeli, Benjamin **4**, 44, 45, 48,
  100; speech (1871) 15
divine right 56
domestic policies, Bismarck's
  (1871-90) **18-19**, 20-6;
  Wilhelm II's (1890-1914)
  54-5, 56-60
Dortmund 59, 95
Dreadnoughts **72**
Dreikaiserbund (1872) **37**; (1873)
  39, 40, 41, 43; (1881) **38**,
  39-40, 41, 42; (1884)
  39-40, 42
Dresdner Bank 93
Dual Alliance (1879) **37-8**, 39, 40,
  41; quoted 49
Duisburg 59

earnings, average (1871-1913)
  99
eastern front **105**
economic depression (mid-1870s)
  23, 28-9, 91
economic domination 107
economic unity **2**
economy 63-4, 77; and the
  colonies 47, 48; expansion of
  German (1871-1914) 91-4;
  effect on society and politics
  94-7; sources 98-100; post-
  war dislocation 111
education 93; and the Catholic
  Church 21; students in higher
  (1891-1912) 99
Egypt 46, **73**
electoral alliance *see* Kartell
electricity industry 93
Eley, G. 48, 59-60
élites 10, 12, 48, 58, 60, 61, 94,
  95-6, 97, 106, 110, 111;
  failure of traditional 82
employment, and poverty 100-3
Ems telegram **3**, 4
Essen 95
Estonia 82, 107
Eulenburg, Prince Philipp zu **54**,
  61; letter to Bülow (1900)
  68
Evans, R.J. 59-60
expansionism **38**, 74, 81-2, 107

exports, and imports (1880-1913)
  99
Eyck, E. 46-7

Falk, Paul, May Laws (1873, 1874)
  21
Falkenhayn, Erich von 111
fascism 59
Federal Customs Union 6
Ferdinand, Archduke Franz of
  Austria, assassinated in
  Sarajevo (1914) **73**
Fieldhouse 45
Finland **106**
Fischer, F. 56, 58, 74, 78, 81-2,
  85, 106, 107, 110
Fontane, Theodor 26
foreign and colonial policies
  (1871-90), Bismarck's **37-8**,
  39-43
foreign and imperial policies
  (1890-1914), Wilhelm II's
  54-5, **71-4**, 74-80
France 4, 5, 12, 21, **38**, 39, 42,
  43, 64, 80, 81, 83, 107, 109,
  111-12; alliance with Russia
  (1893-94) **71-2**, 75, 76;
  anticlerical policy 22;
  Bismarck isolates 40, 46, 74;
  Britain's relations with (1904)
  72-3, 75; colonies 44, 45-6;
  diplomacy with 6, 39;
  economic domination of 82;
  Germany invades (1914) **73**,
  105; industrialisation 91;
  Opportunists and Radicals
  27; Prussian war with
  (1870-71) **3**, **37**; republican
  laws (1871) 27
Franco-British Entente (1904) **38**,
  72-3, 75, 83
Franco-Russian alliance (1894) 41,
  71-2, **73**, 83, 86
Frankfurt, Treaty of (1871) **3**,
  41
Frankfurt Parliament **2**, 7, 9
Frederick the Great (1740-86) of
  Prussia 7, 78, 84
Friedrich III (1888) **18**, **19**, 24, 25,
  47, 56

Free Conservatives 11, 23, 29, 62, 96
Freisinnige (Independent) Party 24
French Ambassador, Bismarck to the (1885) 52
Freud, Sigmund 69
Friedrich Wilhelm IV 9

Gambetta, Léon 46
Gastein, Convention of (1865) 2, 6
German Confederation 1, 9; dissolved 2, 3
German East Africa 38, 44, 46, 107
German East Africa Company 46
German Empire 3; formation and structure 1–3, 9
Germany, case for aggression 81–2, 85; effect of WWI on 110–13; proclamation of Republic (1918) 112; relationship with Britain 57–8, 72, 75, 76–7; sources on 12–14; surrender of 109; war aims 106–9
Grant Robertson, C. 4
Great Britain see Britain
Greater Germany ambitions 82, 107
Grössere Deutschland, Das 88

Habsburg Empire 109
Hanover 3, 6
Harden, Maximilian, description of the Kaiser 68
Hattingen 59
Herero Uprising (1906) 55, 64
Herwig, H.H. 77
Hesse 3, 6
Hindenburg, Field Marshal von 106, 111, 112, 113, 114–15
historiography, German 56
Hitler, Adolf 78, 85
Hohenlohe-Schillingsfürst, Chlodwig zu (1894–1900) 54, 56, 61, 63, 65, 78; extract from memoirs 51
Hohenzollern 3, 6, 26
Holland 82, 107, 108

Holstein 2, 3, 4, 6, 54, 56, 61, 71, 78
Holy Roman Empire 1
Hungary, revolution against Austria (1848–49) 5

Imperial Chancellor 3
imperial policies (1890–1914), Wilhelm II's 71–4
imperialism 44–6, 46–8, 80
Independent Socialists 112
India 46
individualist approach 56–8
industrial interests 23, 28, 29–30, 54, 55
industrial revolution, in Prussia 8, 91
industrialisation 91–5
industrialists 58, 63, 82, 96
inheritance tax 62
internationalism 97
Italy 5, 27, 28, 37, 63; alliance with (1866) 4; joins Triple Alliance (1882) 38, 39, 40, 41, 46; liberal state (1861) 27; neutrality of 74

Jagow, Gottlieb von 83, 89
Jameson Raid 72
Japan 72
Jesuits 21
Junkers, Prussian 10, 12, 29, 55, 95–6
Jutland, Battle of (1916) 109

Kaiser 3, 10, 11; Bismarck's relations with 24, 47; decline in power 111; power of the 57, 65, 68–9, 78; relations with Chancellors 61
Kaiserreich see German Empire
Kamerun 38, 44, 46
Kartell (electoral alliance) 19, 24–5, 29–30, 43
Kehr, E. 63
Keynes, J.M. 8
kleindeutsch national state 8
Kolonialverein 44–5
Königgratz, battle of (1866) 3
KPD see Communist Party

Kruger, President **72**
Kulturkampf **18**, 21–2, 29; failure of 22, 23, 25, 26, 27, 30, 42, 43; sources 33–4

labour force, distribution of 98
laissez-faire 28–9, 42
landowners, Prussian *see* Junkers, Prussian
Langer, W.L. 40
Lasker 20
Layton, G. 78
League of Three Emperors *see* Dreikaiserbund
Lebensraum 78, 107
legal code **18**, 20
Lerman, K.A. 78
liberalism 7, 9, 10, 11, 27; alliance with nationalism 1–2
Liberals, British 63
Lichnowsky, Prince 89
Lithuania 82, 107
Livonia 82, 107
Lloyd George, David 112
Lorraine **3**, 21; *see also* Alsace-Lorraine
Ludendorff, Erich **106**, 113
Luxembourg 4, 5

Manteuffel, Otto 8; Bismarck's letter to 12–13
Marne, Battle of the (1914) **105**
Masurian Lakes, Battle of (1914) **105**
Max of Baden, Prince **106**, 112
Meinecke, Friedrich 110, 113, 114
Metz, battle of (1870) **3**
middle classes 11, 58, 60, 64, 78, 80, 94, 96–7, 106, 110, 111, 112
Middle East **72**
militarism 78–9, 83–4
military approach 6, 7
military dictatorship **106**, 111–12, 113
military interests, and the law **55**
mining industry 92
Minister President of Prussia **3**
Mommsen, Wolfgang J. 9–10, 11, 12, 27, 44, 57, 83, 91

Morier, Sir Robert 13–14
Morocco (1911) crisis **73**, 75, 77, 81
Mühler, Heinrich von, memorandum to Bismarck (1871) 33–4
Munich uprising (1848) **1**

Napoleon Bonaparte **1**
Napoleon III **3**, 4, 6
Nation, Die 66
National Liberals 11, **18**, **19**, 20, 21, 23, 24, 25, 27, 28–9, 42, 43, 62, 96, 112
National Socialism *see* Nazism
nationalism 12, 97; alliance with liberalism 1–2
Nationalists 112
Naumann, Friedrich 68–9
naval expenditure 63, 77–8
naval race with Britain **72**, 76–7, 109
Navy Laws (1897, 1900, 1906) 64, **72**, 75, 78
Nazism 78, 82
Netherlands 27
New Guinea 44
New York Herald 65–6
Nicholas II, Tsar **73**
Norddeutsche Allgemeine Zeitung 57
North Africa 44
North German Confederation **3**, 9, 20, 29

Oberhausen 59
Oberste Heeresleitung (OHL) 111, 112
officer corps 58
Ottoman Empire 109

Pacific Islands **38**, 44
Palmerston, Lord (Henry Temple) 5
Pan-German League 78
pan-Germanism 78, 82, 87
pan-Slavism 80
Panzer divisions 108
patriotism 48, 63, 64, 78, 80, 97, 106, 110
peace **71**
People's Party 112

petty-bourgeoisie 59
Pius IX, Pope 21, 22
Poincaré, Raymond 81
Poland 82, 85, 107
Polish minorities 4, 21, 22
political parties 11, 20–1, 23–5,
    112
political revolution 109, 110
political unity **1–2**
population, growth (1871–1910)
    94, 95, 98
populism 27, 28
Portugal, Anglo-German
    Agreement on colonies
    (1898) **72**
Posadowsky 58, 59, 62
Posen 21
poverty, and employment 100–3
Prague, Treaty of **3**, 4
Progressives 11, 62, 112
progressivism, Prussian 8, 9
proletariat 11, 23, 48, 60, 78, 95
protectionism 29, 42
Protestantism 7, 21
Prussia **1**, 40, 84; annexes
    Schleswig and Holstein **3**;
    constitution (1850) 9;
    economic growth 8, 92;
    expansion of **2**, 7; integration
    into Germany 110; sources
    on 12–14; and unification 4,
    6–8, 77–8; war with Austria
    (1866) **2–3**, 4, **37**; war with
    France **3**, **37**
Prussian Landtag **2**; Army Bill
    debate (1862) 7; Bismarck's
    speech to (1862) 13
public opinion 57, 59, 60, 79
Pulzer, P. 58, 95

Quidde 57

racism 78
railways 81, 84, 108
Raw Materials Department (KRA)
    111
Realpolitik 21
Recklinghausen 59
Reformation 7
Reich Chancellor 10, 11

Reichstag 9, 11, 20, **55**, 58, 60,
    61, 64, 79, **106**; Bismarck's
    speech to the Budget
    Commission (1884) 52;
    Bülow's dissolution (1906)
    64; Centre Party seats
    (1871–90) 34; and
    Chancellors 61, 62; elections
    (1907) 62; elections (1912)
    55
Reinsurance Treaty (1887) **38**, 40,
    41, 43, 46–7, 76; quoted 49;
    Wilhelm II refuses to renew
    (1890) 43, **71**, 75, 78
representative government, spread
    of 27
research 92–3, 94
Retallack, J. 59
revolution (1848) 9
Rhineland 8, 30, 92; southern 6
Ritter 74
Röhl, J.C.G. 57
Romania 82, 107
Romantic movement **1**
Rothfels 9
Ruhr 59, 95
Russell, Lady Emily, description of
    Bismarck 31–2
Russia 4, 5, **37**, **38**, 39, 46, 63,
    64, **71**, 74, 80, 81; alliance
    with France (1893–94) **71–2**,
    75, 76, 83, 86; Bismarck
    courts 40, 46–7; Germany
    declares war on (1914) **73**,
    105–6; tsarist 12; war with
    Turkey **37**
Russian Revolutions (1917)
    105–6

Saarland 6
Sadowa, battle of **3**
Salisbury, Lady 13–14
Salisbury, Lord, Bismarck's letter
    to (1887) 49–50
Sammlungspolitik 29–30, 48, 58
Samoan Islands **72**
Sarajevo, Archduke Ferdinand
    assassinated (1914) **73**, 79,
    81, 82
Saxony **3**, 7; King of 66

Scheidemann, Philipp, speech
(1918) 114
Schellendorff, Bronsart von 31
Schiffer (National Liberal Party) 88
Schleswig 2, 3, 4, 6
Schlieffen, Alfred, Graf von 64
Schlieffen Plan (1914) 73, 84, 85,
105, 107-8
Second Reich 10, 28-9, 85, 113;
authoritarianism of 9-12;
ended (1918) 109; executive
10-11; legislature 11
Sedan, battle of 3
Serbia, Austrian ultimatum to
(1914) 73, 81, 82, 83, 85, 89
Serbs 37
Seven Years War (1756-63) 84
Siemens 93
Siemens-Schukert 93
Silesia 7
smaller German states 2, 6
Social Darwinism 78
Social Democratic Party (SPD) 11,
18, 19, 24, 25, 27, 42, 43,
54-5, 58, 60, 64, 79, 95,
106; formed (1875) 22;
growth (1890-1912) 62;
majority in Reichstag elections
(1912) 55; split 97, 112;
support for (1877-1890) 23,
26, 30; support for war effort
110; views of the 66
social imperialism 59, 80
social insurance 19, 23, 30, 62-3
social reform 54, 62-3
socialism 22-3, 27, 29, 37, 42, 97
south German states 3, 4, 6-7, 10
South West Africa 38, 44, 46, 55,
64, 107
South West Africa Company 46
Sozialdemokrat 23
Spahn, Martin 87
Spanish candidature, Wilhelm I's
telegram on 3, 4
Spartacists 97, 112
SPD see Social Democratic Party
steel production 91
structuralist approach 56, 58-60,
77-8
submarine warfare 109

Sudetenland, Hitler annexes
(1939) 85
Suez Canal 46
Sybel, Heinrich von 21; on
Bismarck 14

Tag, Der 87
tanks 108
Tannenberg, Battle of (1914) 105,
108
tariffs, agricultural 63; introduction
of (1879) 18, 23-4, 28, 29,
93; reduction of (1890) 54
Taylor, A.J.P. 4, 41, 46, 47
Technical High Schools 93
telegram, from Wilhelm I of Prussia
which Bismarck rewrote
(1870) 3, 4
textile industry 92
Third Reich 85
Thomson, D. 45
Tirpitz, Admiral Alfred von 54, 56,
61, 72, 76, 79; advice to
Wilhelm II 86-7
Togoland 38, 44, 46
Townsend, M.E. 44
Treitschke, Heinrich von 15
trench warfare 105, 108
Triple Alliance (1882) 38, 39, 40,
41, 46, 76
Triple Entente (1907) 83
Tunisia 46
Turkey 82, 107; Russian war with
37

Uganda 44
Ukraine 106
unification 28, 110; Bismarck's
'steering' 19, 20, 84;
chronology 2-3; and
colonialism 44-5; issues in
4-8, 77-8
unionism 95
United Kingdom see Britain
United States 45, 93, 96; enters
war (1917) 105, 109

Verdun, Battle of (1916) 105
Versailles, proclamation of German
Empire (1871) 1

Versailles, Treaty of (1919) 65;
    Article 231 on German
    responsibility 81
Vienna, Congress of (1815) 1, 8,
    92; Treaty of (1864) 2
Vienna uprising (1848) 1
von der Heydt 8

Wahre Jacob, Der, cartoon 102
Waldersee, General von 86
war, Clausewitz on 78–9, 84
'War Council' (1912) 82, 84
wealth, poverty and employment
    100–3
Weber, Max 10
Wehler, H.–U. 9, 48, 58, 59, 69,
    74, 80, 83
Weimar Republic 106, 112, 113
welfare legislation (1900–08)
    58–9, 62–3, 64
Weltpolitik 63, 65, 72, 75, 77–8,
    79, 82, 97, 107
West Prussia 21, 30
western front 105
Westphalia 8
Wilhelm I (1871–88) 2, 18; and
    Bismarck 19, 24, 42–3, 47,
    56, 61; 'New Era' 9; speech
    to Prussian Council of
    Ministers (1871) 33; telegram
    which Bismarck rewrote
    (1870) 3
Wilhelm II (1888–1918) 12, 18,
    19, 23, 25, 43; character and
    power, sources 68–9;

conversation on Austrian
    ultimatum to Serbia 89;
    domestic policies
    (1890–1914) 54–5, 56–60;
    foreign and imperial policies
    (1890–1914) 71–4, 74–80;
    proclamation (1914) 113–14;
    relations with Bismarck 56;
    speech to army recruits
    (1891) 68; telegram to
    Caprivi 66
Wilhelmine Germany (1890–1918)
    30, 54–5, 56–65
'Wilhelminism' 58
Williamson, D.G. 46
Windthorst 23, 25, 26, 65–6
working class 11, 18–19, 25, 27,
    30, 55, 58, 59–60, 63, 64,
    79, 94, 95, 97, 106, 110,
    111
World War I (1914–18) 105–6;
    attitudes in Germany to,
    sources 113–15; effect on
    Germany 110–13; outbreak
    55, 62, 71, 74; German
    responsibility for 80–5;
    sources 88–90
World War II (1939–45), compari-
    son 85
Württemberg 3, 6, 7, 10

Zabern Affair (1913) 55, 57, 65
Zanzibar 44
Zollverein 2, 8, 92
Zukunft, Die 68